Constitution of India

अ अक्षर
प्रतियोगी पुस्तकें

Constitution of India

The Prime Minster in his mantra for the Constitution Day gave a new meaning to KYC

Dr. Subhash C. Kashyap

RAJKAMAL

ISBN: 978-93-94902-34-3

Price: ₹125

First Edition: 2022

Published by Rajkamal Prakashan Pvt. Ltd.
1-B, Netaji Subhash Marg
New Delhi-110 002

Branches: Ashok Rajpath, Near Science College, Patna-800 006
Ist Floor, Darbari Building, Mahatama Gandhi Marg, Prayagraj-211 001
36 A, Shekspear Sarni, Kolkata-700 017

Website: www.rajkamalprakashan.com
Email: info@rajkamalprakashan.com

Printed at: B.K. Offset
Naveen Shahadara, Delhi-32

CONSTITUTION OF INDIA
by Dr. Subhash C. Kashyap

Preface

The title of this work is inspired by the Prime Minister's invocation to the people on the last Constitution Day (26 November, 2020). KYC is a popular dictum in the corporate sector but the Prime Minister gave it a new meaning: "Know Your Constitution".

Democracy, freedom and free institutions cannot, for long, survive if we, the people, do not know the system under which we are governed. It is imperative that we discharge our responsibilities and perform our duties as citizens of a free nation. The Constitution of India makes it the first "fundamental duty of every citizen to abide by the Constitution and respect its ideals and institutions." (Article 51A)

For some 65 years now, in all humility, we have been carrying on a civil campaign to spread constitutional literacy in the country. Apart from the work on the 6-volume IIPA project on the 'Framing of India's Constitution' and the founding of the Institute of Constitutional and Parliamentary Studies, I have been writing and speaking a great deal (perhaps too much) on the Constitution of India and allied topics. In addition to the 3-volume study on the 'Constitutional Law of India' (Universal/LexisNexis) and the popular NBT (National Book Trust) bestseller 'Our Constitution', I can brag about several other prestigious titles including two NBT booklets to serve as primers for neo-literates.

In that context and in view of my years (92 plus) and also perhaps because I was naturally afraid of repeating myself, I was very reluctant to to agree to Shri Ashok Maheshwariji's (Rajkamal Prakashan) proposal to prepare another short book on the Constitution. Also, I sent to him some of my books which, I thought, already covered the desired ground. However, he would not relent. The result is before you. I hope that this would be seen as one more effort by Rajkamal Prakashan in the direction of spreading basic awareness of the Constitution of India, its ideals and institutions.

Recently, I was asked to prepare a short advisory note for law students on studying the Constitution. That is being reproduced here after the last chapter as an addendum.

The original calligraphed copy of the Constitution, signed by all the members of the Constituent Assembly, is being preserved carefully in a strong room in Parliament Library. Another copy is kept in the National Archives. The historical illustrations given here at the beginning of each chapter are reproductions of the famous artist Nand Lal Bose's decorations and illuminations on the calligraphed sheets.

Criticism, comments and suggestions for improvement shall be welcome.

26 November, 2021 **—Dr. Subhash C. Kashyap**

Content

1. Constitution — 11
   Meaning and Role
2. Constitution of India — 14
   Constituent Assembly and Constitution Making
3. Constitution Making since 1950 — 22
   Constitutional Amendments (1950-2021)
4. Preamble — 26
   The Soul of the Constitution
5. Union and it's Territory — 37
6. Citizenship of India — 40
7. Fundamental Rights and Directive Principals of State Policy — 44
8. Fundamental Duties of Every Citizen — 52
9. Structure of Indian Polity — 58
   The Union Executive and Legislature
10. Judiciary — 64
11. State Executive and Legislature — 76
12. Union-State Relations — 81
13. Emergency Provisions — 86
14. Elections — 91
15. Local Self-Government Institutions — 94
    Panchayati Raj
16. Unique Features of India's Constitution — 98

Annexure — **102**
Table of Constitutional Amendments (1950-2021)

Addendum — **121**
Studying The Constitution

Constitution of India

1

Constitution

Meaning and Role

Literally, 'constitution' means what constitutes a body, what are its main parts or how it is organised. Every organised body—association, club, society or State needs some basic rules—with whatever name it is called—in regard to its objectives, structure and functioning. In case of States, the need is more pronounced. In western political thought, the concept of a State Constitution is usually traced back to Aristotle's *Politics* and *Constitution of Athens*. In modern times, in cases of societies committed to democratic and liberal views, the first exercise of their sovereign power by a free people is usually to give themselves a constitution. The Constitution constitutes the basic law of the nation. On it's anvil, all other laws and executive acts are tested for their validity and legitimacy. The Constitution lays down the foundational principles and the structure of the political system under which the people decide to govern themselves. The Constitution of a country establishes the three main organs of the State—the Executive, the Legislature and the Judiciary—and lays down the ground rules under which they have to function and exercise the powers entrusted to them. Their jurisdictional limits, relationship with each other and with the people are clearly defined and demarcated by the Constitution.

The fundamental rights and citizenship obligations of the people themselves are also laid down by the Constitution. Next to the people themselves, the Constitution is supreme in polity. In a federal situation or where political powers are distributed between two or more tiers of government, the Constitution also delineates their respective spheres—between the Union, Central or Federal level on the one hand and those at the level of States, Provinces or units on the other.

Looked at from another angle, it is wrong to regard a country's Constitution as a mere inert document or only as a book containing the text of the provisions of the Constitution. The Constitution is not a lifeless thing, it is a living organism of functioning institutions. It is a dynamic reality which keeps constantly growing, evolving. Every Constitution gets meaning and content only from the manner in which, and the people by whom it is operated, what amendments are made, the effects it acquires from how it is interpreted by the courts of the land and the conventions and practices that grow around it in the actual process of its working.

Types of Constitutions

There may be many variants or types of constitutions of nations. Constitutions may be, broadly speaking, written or unwritten. The classic example of the written model is the U.S. Constitution of 1787 while the U.K. Constitution represents the unwritten model. The U.S. Constitution is said to be the first written Constitution of the modern world. Constitutions may be called rigid or flexible on the ground of the amending process being difficult or easy. Constitutions are sometimes also divided between federal and unitary. Federal constitutions are usually classified as rigid because of their rigid amending procedure.

Evaluation

Whether the Constitution proves to be good and successful depends very much on:

1. whether it is suited to the ethos, background and needs of the country;
2. whether the men and women who are called upon to work the Constitution are persons of character and calibre and willing to shoulder their constitutional duties and citizenship responsibilities; and
3. whether the different organs, institutions and functionaries of the State adhere to to their assigned roles and not cross their jurisdictional limits.

2

Constitution of India

Constituent Assembly and Constitution Making

The 15th of August is celebrated every year as the day of India's Independence from nearly 200 years of British colonial rule. As the clock struck 12 on the midnight of 14-15 August 1947, sovereign power was formally transferred from British to Indian hands. We had to pay a very heavy price for the dawn of Independence. India was partitioned. Apart from the countless supreme sacrifices made during the long freedom struggle, we had to face mass uprooting, killing and transfer of populations on both sides of the divide. Independent India had myriads of problems, many of them stupendous. 15 August, 1947 was not the journey's end, struggle for freedom had to continue on several fronts. The President of the Constituent Assembly, Dr. Rajendra Prasad addressing the Assembly in his poetic prose appealed to his countrymen at large, and members of the Constituent Assembly in particular, to get down in right earnest to the task of building the future India of their dreams. He said:

> "Making a new Constitution for India—first Constitution of the people, by the people and for the people of India—was one of the most formidable and challenging tasks.

The Constituent Assembly had to frame a Constitution for a country with the second largest population in the world and with myriad linguistic, regional, religious and other diversities. It had to tackle many fundamental issues. On their satisfactory resolution depended the entire future of the new nation. Also, the Constitution framed by the Assembly had to be worthy of a great people, rooted in their glorious past and suited to their future aspirations. Apart from the difficulties inherent in framing a Constitution for a country of the size, population and diversity of India, during the first 78 months of its existence the Constituent Assembly had to function in a setting of acute political uncertainties and widespread communal violence. Even after the main issue of partition had been finally settled under the 3 June plan, there was the tremendous problem of bringing into the Dominion of India the 552 Princely States situated within the geographical limits of the Dominion and then, of integrating them into the constitutional structure of a democratic and structure of a democratic and republican India. However, undaunted by the difficulties and baffling problems faced by them, the leaders of the Indian revolution went ahead with the task of Constitution-making."

In law, sovereign powers in India were transferred to the Constituent Assembly which had been already set up under the British Cabinet Mission Plan and was engaged in the Constitution-making exercise since 9 December, 1946 even though the Muslim League members continued to abstain. The first important job for the Constituent Assembly was to discuss the resolution on Aims and Objects of the Constitution for free India. The resolution often called 'The Objectives Resolution' was moved by Jawaharlal Nehru. From 12 December to

19 December, 1946, the Assembly debated at length on the Objectives Resolution. A large number of amendments were tabled, but the debate centred round an amendment which sought postponement of the discussion on the Resolution until the Muslim League and representatives of Princely States joined the deliberations of the Assembly. Further discussion on the Resolution was postponed on 21 December, 1946 until the House reassembled for the next session. The Muslim League had a full month to consider the matter, but they did not choose to come in. The Assembly, thereafter, declined to wait any further and 'remembering the solemnity of the occasion and the greatness of the pledge and the promise which the resolution contained'. It adopted the Resolution on 22 January, 1947 in a solemn manner, all members standing.

Soon after, the Assembly appointed a number of committees to deal with different aspects of the problem of framing the Constitution. These included, the Union Constitution Committee. Provincial Constitution Committee, Union Powers Committee, Committee on Fundamental Rights, Minorities etc. Some of these Committees were headed by either Nehru or Patel to whom the President of the Assembly gave the credit for working out the fundamentals of the Constitution. The Committees worked hard and in a business like manner and produced valuable reports.

The first draft of the Constitution of India, known as the Constitutional Advisor's Draft was prepared in October 1947, by the Advisory Branch of the Office of the Constituent Assembly. Before the preparation of this draft, voluminous background material had been collected and supplied to the members of the Assembly in the shape of three series of Constitutional Precedents which gave, among other things, some executive, legislative, procedural and administrative provisions as well as some other salient texts from constitutions of about 60 countries. The Constitutional Precedents also contained background material in respect of the Head of the State, Fundamental Rights, Safeguards for Minorities, Systems of Representation and Second Chambers in various countries.

After the first draft of the Constitution of India had been prepared, the Constitutional Adviser, B.N. Rau, was deputed by the President of the Assembly to visit U.S.A., Canada, Eire and Britain for personal discussions on important features of India's draft constitution with leading constitutional experts. He visited these countries between October and December 1947 and submitted a report embodying the results of the discussions.

After a general discussion of the reports of some of the important Committees, the Constituent Assembly, by a resolution, adopted on 29 August, 1947, appointed the Drafting Committee with Dr. B.R. Ambedkar as the Chairman to scrutinize the draft of the text of the Constitution of India prepared by the Constitutional Adviser giving effect to the decisions taken in the Assembly and including all matters which were ancillary thereto or which had to be provided in such a Constitution, and to submit to the Assembly for consideration the text of the draft Constitution as revised by the Drafting Committee.

The Draft Constitution of India prepared by the Drafting Committee was submitted to the President of the Assembly on 21 February, 1948. Since a large number of comments, criticisms and suggestions for the amendment of the Draft Constitution were received in the office of the Constituent Assembly, the President of the Assembly directed the Drafting Committee to consider all these. He also constituted a Special Committee consisting mostly of the members of the Union Constitution Committee, the Provincial Constitution Committee and the Union Powers Committee, to go through the comments and suggestions received along with the recommendations of the Drafting Committee thereon. The Special Committee met and made certain recommendations. As a result of this examination the Drafting Committee picked out some amendments which it would like to support and also suggested certain others which it would like to recommend. To facilitate reference to such amendments the Drafting Committee decided to issue a reprint of the Draft Constitution which was submitted to the President of the Assembly on 26 October, 1948. It was subsequently circulated to members of the Constituent Assembly and used when the Draft Constitution was placed before the Assembly for consideration. In this reprint of the Draft Constitution the amendments recommended for adoption by the Drafting Committee were shown in the second column opposite the clauses or the articles which they sought to amend. While introducing the Draft Constitution in the Assembly for consideration on 4 November, 1948, Dr. Ambedkar replied to some common criticisms of the Draft, particularly the criticism in regard to there being very little in it that could claim originality. He observed:

> "One likes to ask whether there can be anything new in a Constitution framed at this hour in the history of the world. More than 100 years have rolled over when the first written Constitution was drafted. It has been followed by many countries reducing their Constitutions to writing. What the scope of a Constitution should be has long been settled. Similarly what are the fundamentals of a Constitution are recognised all over the world. Given these facts, all Constitutions in their main provisions must look similar. The only new things, if there can be any, in a Constitution framed so late in the day are the variations made to remove the faults and to accommodate it to the

> needs of the country. The charge of producing a blind copy of the Constitutions of other countries is based, I am sure, on an inadequate study of the Constitution. As to the accusation that the Draft Constitution had produced a good part of the provisions of the Government of India Act, 1935, I make no apologies. There is nothing to be ashamed of in borrowing. It involves no plagiarism. Nobody holds any patent rights in the fundamental ideas of a Constitution."

The clause-by-clause consideration of the Draft Constitution commenced on 15 November, 1948. Following the procedure adopted in case of bills in the House of Commons, it was decided to consider the Preamble after considering all the clauses of the Draft Constitution. The Second Reading of the Constitution was completed on 16 November, 1949 and on the next day the Assembly took up the Third Reading of the Constitution, with a motion by Dr. Ambedkar 'that the Constitution as settled by the Assembly be passed'. The motion was adopted on 26 November, 1949 and thus on that day, the people of India in their Constituent Assembly adopted, enacted and gave to themselves the Constitution of the Sovereign Democratic Republic of India. The Chairman of the Drafting Committee, Dr. Ambedkar and the President of the Assembly, Dr. Rajendra Prasad speaking on 25 and 26 November, 1949 sounded words of warning and wisdom. Dr. Ambedkar said:

> "I feel, however good a Constitution may be, it is sure to turn out bad because those who are called to work it, happen to be a bad lot. However bad a Constitution may be, it may turn out to be good if those who are called to work it, happen to be a good lot. The working of a Constitution does not depend wholly upon the nature

of the Constitution. The Constitution can provide only the organs of State such as the legislature, the executive and the judiciary. The factor on which the working of those organs of State depends are the people and the political parties they will set up as their instruments to carry out their wishes and their politics. Who can say how the people of India and their parties will behave?

... In addition to our old enemies in the form of castes and creeds, we are going to have many political parties with diverse and opposing political creeds. Will Indians place the country above their creed or will they place creed above country? I do not know. But this much is certain that if the parties place creed above country, our independence will be put in jeopardy a second time and probably be lost for ever. This eventuality we must all resolutely guard against. We must be determined to defend our independence with the last drop of our blood."

Dr. Rajendra Prasad in his concluding speech observed that they had been able, on the whole, to draft a good Constitution which he trusted would serve the country well. But, he added:

"If the people who are elected are capable and men of character and integrity, they would be able to make the best even of a defective Constitution. If they are lacking in these, the Constitution cannot help the country. After all, a Constitution like a machine is a lifeless thing. It acquires life because of the men who control it and operate it, and India needs today nothing more than a set of honest men who will have the interest of the country before them. There is a fissiparous tendency arising out of various elements in our life. We have communal differences, caste differences, language differences, provincial differences and so forth. It requires men of strong character, men of vision, men who will not sacrifice the interests of the country at large for the sake of smaller groups and areas and who will rise over the prejudices which are born of these differences. We can only hope that the country will throw up such men in abundance."

3

Constitution Making since 1950

Constitutional Amendments (1950-2021)

A point may need to be reiterated here: Constitution at work is not something inert or static. It is a living, dynamic process of functioning institutions. A living Constitution is ever in the making through the ways it is worked, the type of persons by whom it worked and the amendments that are made by Parliament and the way these are interpreted by the courts. Secondly, article 368 of the Constitution makes it very clear that the constituent power—the power to make or amend the Constitution—vests entirely in the Union Parliament when it says that, "Notwithstanding anything in this Constitution, Parliament may in exercise of its constituent power amend by way of addition, variation or repeal any provision of the Constitution…," and adds that ". . . An amendment of this Constitution may be initiated ONLY by introduction of a Bill for the purpose in either House of Parliament. . ."

Thomas Jefferson, one of the makers of the Constitution of the United States believed that each generation could be considered a separate nation: "with a right by the will of the majority to bind themselves, but none to bind the succeeding generation, more than the inhabitants of another country". Our founding fathers also realised that the people in each generation enjoy the same sovereign powers of deciding how and by whom they should be governed and that they could not bind the succeeding generations irretrievably against their sovereign will. They provided, therefore, for a largely flexible procedure for amending the provisions of the Constitution to suit the changing needs of the society. Also, for this purpose they vested in Parliament constituent powers on a continuing basis. Our present Constitution—the first Constitution of India proclaimed by its Preamble to have been framed by 'We, the people of India' themselves came into full operation with effect from 26 January, 1950. It has been growing ever since. Constitution-making has continued. Article 368 of the Constitution is the specific provision dealing with amendment of the Constitution. First, an amendment of the Constitution can be initiated only by the introduction of a Bill in either House of Parliament. Thus the initiative in the matter of constitutional amendment has been exclusively reserved for Parliament. Second, most of the provisions of the Constitution can be amended By Parliament only by a special majority, namely, a majority of the total membership as well as a majority of not less than two-thirds of the members of each House present and voting. It is only in the case of a limited category of constitutional provisions, (i.e., those relating to the Election of the President, Executive power of the Union and the States, Judiciary, the Lists in the Seventh Schedule, representation of States in Parliament, provisions of article 368, etc.) that the Amendment Bill, having been passed by each House of Parliament with the prescribed special majority, needs to be ratified by the legislatures of not less than one-half of the States. Third, on a Constitution Amendment Bill, as duly passed/ratified, being presented to the President, the President's assent is mandatory and, unlike in the case of ordinary legislative Bills, he has no option of withholding his assent or returning the Bill to the Houses for re-consideration. And, lastly, it is significant that none of the provisions of the Constitution is unamendable inasmuch as Parliament can in any way amend, alter or repeal any provision of the Constitution and such amendments cannot be questioned in any court of law on any ground whatsoever unless they tend to alter or violate what may be considered as the basic structure or features of the Constitution.

The present state of the doctrine of basic features is that so long as the decision in the Kesavananda case is not overturned by a larger Bench of the Supreme Court, any amendment to the Constitution is liable to be reviewed by the Court on the ground of affecting one or other of the basic features of the Constitution.

Since the commencement of the Constitution in 1950, the 104 Constitutional Amendments have been brought about under article 368 alone. Without getting into the controversy of the difference between the 'constituent power' vis-a-vis 'amending power', it may be said that this has been done in exercise of the Parliament's powers under article 368. Of the 104 formal Constitutional Amendments effected so far, not all can be considered equally important or of substantial consequence. The more wide-ranging and covering a vast number of provisions and/or the more significant were the seventh, the forty-second, the forty-fourth, the fifty. Second, the seventy-third and the seventy-fourth, the eighty-sixth, the ninety-first and the hundred-first amendments. Some of the Amendments were very minor, merely clarificatory or consequential in nature, some were related to abolition of zamindari, land reforms and property clauses, giving primacy to directive principles or protecting reform laws and regulations by including them in the Ninth Schedule. Several Amendments became necessary for safeguarding the interests of the Scheduled Castes, Scheduled Tribes, Backwards and Minorities, for every ten years extending reservations for the next ten years. A few Amendments were for admitting new territories—like Dadra and Nagar Haveli, Goa, Daman and Diu, Sikkim and Puducherry.

(For the Table on 104 Amendments see the Annexure).

4

Preamble

WE, THE PEOPLE OF INDIA, having solemnly resolved to constitute India into a '[SOVEREIGN SOCIALIST SECULAR DEMOCRATIC REPUBLIC] and to secure to all its citizens:

JUSTICE, social, economic and political;

LIBERTY of thought, expression, belief, faith and worship;

EQUALITY of status and of opportunity; and to promote among them all

FRATERNITY assuring the dignity of the individual and the **[unity and integrity of the Nation];

IN OUR CONSTITUENT ASSEMBLY this twenty-sixth day of November, 1949, do HEREBY ADOPT, ENACT AND GIVE TO OURSELVES THIS CONSTITUTION.

The Soul of the Constitution

The word 'preamble' means what precedes or comes first. In the text of the Constitution of India , the Preamble comes first and precedes all other provisions. It was actually the Objectives Resolution passed by the Constituent Assembly earlier that took the form of the Preamble.

For some time, the Supreme Court mistakenly held the view that the Preamble is not a part of the Constitution. Later, noting that like all other provisions of the Constitution, the Preamble was specifically voted 'to stand part of the Constitution', the Supreme Court revised it's view and declared that the Preamble was the ' key' to the mind of the makers and was 'an epitome' of the broad features of the Constitution.

The Preamble to the Constitution embodies the fundamental values and the philosophy on which it is based and the aims and objectives which the founding fathers—speaking for the people—enjoined the polity to strive to achieve. In Golak Nath vs. State of Punjab, Subba Rao J. said that the objective, sought to be achieved by the Constitution, is declared in sonorous terms in its preamble. It contains in a nutshell, its ideals and its aspirations. The Preamble is not a platitude. The mode of its realisation is worked out in detail in the Constitution.

The Preamble to our Constitution serves several important purposes. First, it indicates the source from which the Constitution comes, viz., the people of India. Next, it contains the enacting clause which brings into force the Constitution. In the third place, it declares the great rights and freedoms which the people of India intended to secure to all citizens and the basic type of government and polity which was sought to be established.

The Preamble can be viewed in two parts—the nature of polity and the objectives of polity. In the first part, it speaks of the values of sovereignty, socialism, secularism, democracy, and republicanship as the characteristics of Indian polity. In the second, it guarantees values of Justice—social, economic and political; Liberty of thought, expression, belief, faith and worship; Equality of status and opportunity; and to promote among all the citizens Fraternity assuring the dignity of the individual and the unity and integrity of the nation. If Justice, Liberty, Equality and Fraternity, including social, economic and political justice, the golden goals set out in the Preamble of the Constitution, are to be achieved, 'the Indian polity has to be educated and educated with excellence'. The concepts and terms that emerge from the text of the Preamble may be analysed as follows:

We, the People

The Preamble speaks of 'We, the People of India' giving, 'to ourselves this Constitution'. Thus, the Preamble serves the purpose of declaring that 'The People of India' are the source of the Constitution and that sovereignty in Indian polity vests in the people. The Constitution of India does not contain any specific provision in regard to the vesting of sovereign powers. The only place from where the residence of sovereignty and the, source of the Constitution itself can be ascertained is the Preamble. The words 'We the People' remind us of the opening words of the Preamble of the U.S. Constitution. But, the Preamble in the U.S. Constitution speaks in the name of 'We, the People of United States'. Its earlier drafts and history make it amply clear that the framers of the American Constitution were referring to the people of the several (13) independent States seeking 'a more perfect union' and not to one people of a nation. The Preamble to the Constitution o India, on the other hand, did not talk of the people of the States of the India Union. Unlike the U.S. Constitution, our Constitution did not even require any ratification by the State. By saying that 'We, the People of India' adopt, enact and give to ourselves this Constitution', the founding fathers solemnly affirmed that we were one people, people of India, and not people of different State etc., that sovereignty belonged to the whole people of India and not to those of separate States and that the Constitution was framed and adopted not by the people of States but by the whole people of India in their collective capacity as one indivisible sovereign unit. It was sought to be stressed that we were one nation and had one Constitution and one polity.

The Preamble, as adopted by the Constituent Assembly, spoke of 'We, the People of India', making a solemn resolve to constitute India into a 'Sovereign Democratic Republic' securing for all its citizens justice, liberty and equality, and promoting fraternity among them all. Justice, is further defined as social, economic and political. Liberty includes liberty of thought, expression, belief, faith and worship, and equality means equality of status and of opportunity.

Infact, Justice, Liberty, Equality and Fraternity are the most essential concomitants of a truly democratic order and therefore, only elucidate the concept of a democratic republic. The ultimate goal is that of 'securing the dignity of the individual and unity of the nation.' Thus, the Preamble serves the purpose of declaring that 'The people of India' are the source of the Constitution, that Sovereignty in Indian polity vests in the people and that Indian Polity is democratic with Fundamental Rights and freedoms guaranteed to all the people and amity among the people and dignity of the individual and integrity and unity of the nation assured.

According to the text of the Preamble as it stood after the 42nd amendment in 1976, the supreme or fundamental constitutional values in which the founding fathers believed, which they wanted to foster among the people of the Republic and which, they hoped, would guide all those who, from generation to generation, were called upon to work the Constitution were:

* Sovereignty
* Socialism
* Liberty
* Equality

* Secularism
* Democracy
* Republican Character
* Justice
* Fraternity
* Dignity of the Individual, and
* Unity and Integrity of the Nation.

Sovereignty

Sovereignty is considered to be one of the essential attributes of a State and connotes absolute and supreme power not subject to control by any internal or external authority. In this traditional sense of sovereignty, no State today can be said to be fully sovereign. Membership of international organisations like the United Nations, European Union, etc. and international treaties, accords and conventions cast obligations, put restraints and erode sovereignty. Another aspect of sovereignty that has been made clear as a value enshrined in the Constitution is that sovereignty vests in the people. It is 'We, the people' who are sovereign and who have given 'to ourselves this Constitution'. No one should forget that the highest functionaries of the State are the creatures of the people and accountable to them. The end objective of the exercise of any power in polity by anyone must be good governance and the good of the people.

Socialism

The Preamble of our Constitution gives almost the highest place of honour to the objective of `Socialism'. It is mentioned next only to 'Sovereign'. However; the term 'Socialism' has not been defined by the Constitution. Dictionary meaning of the word would imply, in full and in part, placing means of production and distribution in public hands, i.e. under public (meaning 'State') Ownership and free enterprises. A relevant question, however, is whether the economic policy of liberalisation, free market competition, privatisation, etc. can be considered socialistic.

Secularism

Often, in our common parlance, the term secularism is used merely as an opposite of 'communalism'. A secular State deals with the individual as a citizen irrespective of his religion. It is not connected to a particular religion nor does it seek to promote or interfere with religion. A secular State attempts to secure the good of all its citizens irrespective of their religious beliefs and practices. It is neutral or impartial in extending its benefits to citizens of all castes and creeds. The meaning sought to be given to the term has been that of *Sarva Dharma Sambhava*, i.e. treating all religions alike or giving equal respect to all religions, instead of *Dharma Nirpeksha* or *Pantha Nirpeksha*, i.e. State neutrality in matters of religion. The Constitution envisaged a new social order free from communal conflicts and based on Justice—social, economic and political. It visualised a polity under which laws would not discriminate between citizens on grounds of religion, caste or the like. The Constitution sought to establish a 'secular' order under which the majority of the population did not enjoy any special privileges or preferential treatment at the hands of the State and 'religious' rights of the minorities were protected in different ways.

Democracy

The basic postulates of Democracy are that the sovereign power resides in the people, that irrespective of religion, caste, creed, colour or sex, all are equal in the eyes of law. Democracy implies that the people govern themselves through their chosen representatives.

There are many variants of democracy which can be considered equally representative and legitimate. We have adopted what is called 'parliamentary democracy'. The founding fathers tried to provide for the fullest representation by enfranchising all the vast adult population of the country without any literacy, property, income tax, or sex criteria. This is borne out by the provisions for universal adult franchise with all adults having the right to vote and the executive being responsible to the popular house of the legislature. For our founding fathers, democracy did not mean merely political democracy or the people's right to periodically vote to elect their representatives. Without social and economic democracy, political democracy had no meaning in a poor country like India. For Dr. Ambedkar, social and economic democracy was the real aim and ultimate goal. He said that 'parliamentary democracy was meaningless unless it was geared to achieving the real goal of economic democracy.' Jawaharlal Nehru also observed that democracy of his conception was only a means to an end. The end was the good life for the individual which must include a certain satisfaction of the essential economic needs.

Republican Character

The concept of 'Republic' is that of a State in which the people are supreme; there is no privileged class and all public offices are open to every citizen without any distinction of race, caste, sex or creed. There is no hereditary ruler and the head of the State is elected by the people for a fixed term. He is usually called the President of the Republic. A Republic is a State in which the supreme power rests in the people and not with a single individual. Democratic Republic may, therefore, broadly means a State with an elected head and a government by the representatives of the people.

It is in the widest sense that the Preamble speaks of India being a Republic. The head of the Union is a President who is elected for a fixed term by an electoral college of the representatives of the people. All citizens are equal in the eyes of law.

Justice

The Preamble promises justice to all citizens. Justice means harmonisation of interests between the individuals, between groups and between the individuals and groups, on the one hand, and interests of the community on the other. Most significantly, the Preamble places Justice higher than the other principles of Liberty, Equality and Fraternity. Justiceis defined or elaborated as social, economic and political, again giving precedence to social and economic over political justice. Social justice implies that all citizens are treated equally irrespective of their status in society as a result of the accident of birth, race, caste, religion, sex, title, etc. Economic justice would require that the rich and the poor are treated alike and that efforts are made to bridge the gap between them. Political justice means equal share to all citizens in the right to participation in the political process without any distinction of race, caste, creed, religion or place of birth.

Founding fathers like Nehru and Ambedkar were quite clear in their minds that political justice was meaningless without economic justice. In our society ridden with religious, caste and creed discriminations, even economic justice was not enough unless it was coupled with social justice. Dr. Ambedkar had said:

> "On 26th January 1950, we are going to enter into a life of contradictions. In politics, we will have equality

> and in social and economic life we will have inequality. In politics, we will be recognising the principle of one man one vote and one vote one value. In our social and economic life, we shall, by reason of our social and economic structure, continue to deny the principle of one man one value."

Liberty

Liberty in the Preamble to our Constitution does not mean mere absence of restraint or domination, it is a positive concept of the right to 'liberty of thought, expression, belief, faith and worship'. It comprehends various freedoms later concretised in the Fundamental Rights part of the Constitution and considered essential for the development of the individual and the nation.

Equality

The concept of Equality embodied in our Preamble is only that of equality of status and opportunity. This has legal, social, political and economic aspects. All citizens are equal before law and enjoy equal protection of the laws of the land. There can be no discrimination between one person and another only on the ground of religion, race, caste, sex, or place of birth in the matter of access to public places and public employment. All citizens are equally entitled to enjoy the political rights to vote and participate in the process of governance without any discrimination. In the economic field, equality means that for the same ability and same labour, the salary would also be the same. Also, one man or one class would not exploit other men or classes.

Fraternity

The ideals of justice, liberty and equality are relevant and meaningful only in as much as these promote a common feeling of brotherhood, of Indian fraternity, of being sons of the same Mother India despite all the racial, linguistic, religious and other diversities of many sorts. Provisions relating to common citizenship are directed towards strengthening Indian fraternal feelings and building a strong Indian fellowship.

In fact, the concept of fraternity is far wider than the concept of secularism. It goes beyond separation of religion and politics, freedom of religion, equal respect for all religions, etc. Unfortunately, not enough importance has been attached by the jurists and judges to this concept. Speaking on the need for the recognition of the principle of fraternity, Dr. Ambedkar remarked in the Constituent Assembly:

> "What does fraternity mean? Fraternity means a sense of common brotherhood of all Indians—of Indians being one people. It is the principle which gives unity and solidarity to social life."

Dignity of the Individual

Fraternity was expected to preserve and promote the dignity of the individual. The unit of Indian polity was the individual citizen. In the minds of the founding fathers, dignity of the individual was of supreme importance. The ultimate objective was to improve the quality of life for the individual, to enable every citizen to live a life of dignity.

Unity and Integrity of the Nation

In order to safeguard the dignity of the individual, we need to build the nation and protect its unity and integrity. It was only through a spirit of common brotherhood and fraternity that we could hope to build national unity in a highly pluralistic society. The highest value in the minds of the framers of the Constitution was to build a united India and a strong and integrated nation from a highly heterogeneous, widely segmented and fragmented feudal society with many diverse pulls of various sorts. Their supreme passion was to demolish all the ugly social barriers of caste and community that divided us and build a common Indian fraternity and fellowship. Also, without unity and integrity of the nation, we could not succeed in our efforts at economic development, nor could we hope to preserve either democracy or the independence of the country and the honour of the countrymen.

5

Union and it's Territory

Article 1(1) begins with the words 'India, that is Bharat'. The question of the name ol the country was discussed in the Constituent Assembly at some length. While 'Bharat' was the ancient name and represented the first expression of the consciousness of the unity and identity of the country, India was the modern name by which the country had since become known all over the world. As a member of the United Nations also the name was India and all international agreements were entered in that name. Both the names, therefore, had strong votaries. Finally, the name 'India, that is Bharat' was adopted as a happy compromise. In the authoritative Hindi version of the Constitution, 'Bharat' comes first when article 1 begins with the words 'Bharat, *arthat* India'.

Union of States

Article 1(1) describes India is a 'Union of States'. The emphasis on India being a 'Union' was to convey the fact that it was not the result of a compact or agreement between the constituent units but a forthright declaration by the Constituent Assembly which derived its power and authority from the sovereign people of India. No State could, therefore, secede from the

Union nor could it *suo motu* vary its territory as laid down in the First Schedule to the Constitution. Article 1(2) refers to the States and territories being as specified in the First Schedule. As in the year 2021, the 28 States and 8 Union Territories are included in the First Schedule. These are:

The States:

1. Andhra Pradesh
2. Arunachal Pradesh
3. Assam
4. Bihar
5. Chhattisgarh
6. Goa
7. Gujarat
8. Haryana
9. Himachal Pradesh
10. Jharkhand
11. Karnataka
12. Kerala
13. Madhya Pradesh
14. Maharashtra
15. Manipur
16. Meghalaya
17. Mizoram
18. Nagaland
19. Odisha
20. Punjab
21. Rajasthan
22. Sikkim
23. Tamil Nadu
24. Telangana
25. Tripura
26. Uttarakhand
27. Uttar Pradesh
28. West Bengal

Union Territories:

1. Andaman and Nicobar Islands
2. Chandigarh
3. Dadra & Nagar Haveli and Daman & Diu
4. Delhi (National Capital Territory)
5. Jammu & Kashmir
6. Ladakh
7. Lakshadweep
8. Puducherry

It may be said that in a classic federation situation it is the independent units (States) that give some of their sovereign powers to the Union while under the scheme of the Constitution of India, it is the indivisible Union that decided to devolve some of its powers to its units. To use Dr. Ambedkar's words, the States were created only for purposes of 'administrative convenience'.

Under Articles 2, 3 and 4 of the Constitution, the name, territory, area, boundary, etc. of any State may be changed by law of the Union Legislature. Also, new States may be admitted to the Union. The political map of India was considerably changed by the amalgamation of princely States, reorganisation of States on linguistic lines, admission of new States like Sikkim and territories like those of Puducherry, Goa, etc. and creation of several new States like those of Haryana, Himachal Pradesh, Nagaland, Manipur, Mizoram, Meghalaya, Jharkhand, Chhattisgarh, Uttarakhand, Telangana, etc.

On the other hand, the existing States may also lose their status. There is the recent case of the State of Jammu & Kashmir being converted into two Union Territories of (1) Jammu & Kashmir and (2) Ladakh.

6

Citizenship of India

Of the 22 Parts of the Constitution of India, a separate Part—Part II—was devoted to citizenship provisions—articles 5 to 11. For the Constituent Assembly and the Drafting Committee this proved to be one of the most difficult parts of the Constitution—making exercise. For 'We, the people of India' the most fundamental consequence for the people of India becoming a Sovereign Democratic Republic was to be at once transformed from the status of 'subjects' of the British to that of 'citizens' of independent India. Under the Government of India Act, 1935 and even till independence, legislatures in India had no power to make nationality laws. Those who lived in British India were under the crown and as such British subjects governed by British Nationality Acts and those who happened to be residing in any of the princely states had the status of British protected persons. Citizenship issue was, therefore, one of the first issues to engage the attention of the Constituent Assembly. The immediate problem was to determine who were the citizens of India at the time of her new status as an independent state in the comity of nations. Article 5 was headlined 'Citizenship on the commencement of the Constitution'. Incidentally, it may be mentioned that it was among the few articles which came into force immediately on the adoption of the Constitution on 26 November, 1949 even though the date of commencement of the Constitution was fixed as 26 January, 1950.

The Constitution does not define the term 'citizen' or 'citizenship'. Citizenship is a legal and political bond and constitutes the indispensable foundational principle of democratic polity. In an organised civil society, the value of citizenship may be said to consist in a combination of rights and duties, privileges and obligations among citizens *inter* se as also in the relationship between the individual citizens and the State authority. Citizenship involves the individual's full political membership in the State, his permanent position of allegiance to the State and the official recognition by the State of his integration into the political system. The Constitution makes a distinction between 'persons' and 'citizens'. Every citizen is a person but every person is not necessarily a citizen or entitled to the status and rights of a citizen. This is made amply clear by Part III of the Constitution on Fundamental Rights. All the fundamental rights guaranteed by the Constitution are available to every citizen but not to aliens who may be residing in the country. Only some of the fundamental rights are extended to all persons e.g., equality before law, right to life and personal liberty, protection against self-incrimination and A double jeopardy, freedom of religion etc. On the other hand, only citizens can hold certain high offices of the state, vote at elections to and be of Union and State Legislatures

Citizenship may also be viewed as the legal relationship between the individual and the State under which the individual pledges his loyalty to the State and State offers its protection to the individual. The relationship is regulated by national law and recognised by international law. It comprises (i) civil and political rights of the citizen which need to be protected by the State even against itself, (ii) duties which the citizen performs towards the State and which include promotion of public good, and (iii) the loyalty of the citizen towards the State. The Constitution of India only laid down the law in regard to citizenship at the commencement of the Constitution. It did not provide for the acquisition and termination of Indian citizenship. Article 11 left it to Parliament to to regulate the right of citizenship by law. Entry 17 in the Union List of the Seventh Schedule of the Constitution also provided for the Union Parliament having the legislative power in the matter of 'citizenship, naturalisation and aliens'. In exercise of its legislative authority conferred by Entry 17 and in pursuance of the provisions of article 11 of Part II, the Parliament passed the Citizenship Act, 1955 which came into force on 30 December, 1955 and provided for acquisition and termination of Indian citizenship. All matters relating to citizenship rights, after the commencement of the Constitution are to be decided in accordance with the provisions of the Act. The Act specifically vests the Union Government with exclusive jurisdiction for determination of all questions of acquisition and loss of Indian Citizenship. The 1955 Citizenship Act has been amended from time to time—in 1981, 1992, 2003, 2005, 2015 and the latest in 2019. Changes have been made in important aspects. Some of the more fundamental ones were those of 2003, 2005 and 2019. Under the 2003 and 2005 Amendments, it was provided *inter alia* that a national register of citizens of India be maintained and certain categories of persons of Indian origin (PIOs) settled abroad (in certain specified countries) be registered as Overseas Citizens of India with facilities like right to buy property, travelling to India without visa, making investments in business etc. but without the right to vote at elections or be candidates for high elective offices. Also, they cannot be appointed to offices of the State like judges or officers in public services. The 2003 Amendment also introduced the notion of 'illegal immigrants' in the citizenship law. The 2019 Citizenship Amendment Act (CAA) provided that those belonging to persecuted minorities—Hindus, Sikhs, Jains, Buddhists and Christians in Pakistan, Afghanistan and Bangladesh who entered India prior to the end of 2014 can be given Indian citizenship. Some elements tried to give a communal colour to CAA by alleging that the Muslims were being singled out and discriminated against in the matter of grant of Indian citizenship.

It was in keeping with the aim of building an integrated Indian nation and a united fraternity that the Constitution-makers decided to provide for a single Indian citizenship with accompanying rights, benefits and obligations throughout the territory of the Union. All citizens, irrespective of the State in which they were born , they are citizens of India and have the same rights and duties all over the country without any discrimination.With the end of the temporary status of the State of Jammu & Kashmir and the application of all the provisions of the Constitution, including the citizenship provisions, to it, the unity and integrity of the nation was further strengthened.

7

Fundamental Rights and Directive Principles of State Policy

Fundamental Rights

One of the most fundamental demands of the leaders of India's national struggle for Independence was that of the people having some basic human rights of freedom, equality, etc. The problems of minorities accentuated the need of having a formal declaration of certain justiciable fundamental rights in the text of the Constitution itself. By and large, the fundamental rights incorporated in Part III of the Constitution are the inviolable rights of the individual against the State. Any law or executive action depriving an individual citizen of his freedom, for example, can be challenged in the Supreme Court or the high courts. It would be held unconstitutional and invalid unless it is covered by any of the restrictions spelled out in the Constitution itself. Thus, the Constitution also lays down the machinery and mechanism for the enforcement of fundamental rights.

Described by Dr. Ambedkar as 'the most criticized part' of the Constitution, Part III dealing with the fundamental rights was discussed for as many as 38 days—11 in the Sub-Committee, 2 in the Advisory Committee and 25 in the Constituent Assembly. Coming closely on the heels of the Universal Declaration of Human Rights (10 December, 1948), inclusion of a bill of rights in the Constitution of India accorded with the contemporary, democratic and humanitarian temper and constitutional practice in other nations of the world.

The fundamental rights have been guaranteed under six broad categories, namely:

(i) The RIGHT TO EQUALITY including EQUALITY BEFORE LAW and the EQUAL PROTECTION OF LAWS (article 14), prohibition of discrimination on grounds of religion, race, caste, sex, or place of birth (article 15), EQUALITY OF OPPORTUNITY in the matters of public employment (article 16); and abolition of untouchability and the system of titles (articles 17 and 18);

(ii) The RIGHT TO FREEDOM including the RIGHT TO (protection of) LIFE AND (personal) LIBERTY (article 21), and the right to freedom of speech and expression, assembly, association or union, movement and to reside and settle in any part of India, and the right to practice any profession or occupation (article 19). Has

(iii) The RIGHT AGAINST EXPLOITATION, prohibiting all forms of FORCED LABOUR, CHILD LABOUR and TRAFFIC IN HUUMAN BEINGS (articles 23and24);

(iv) The RIGHT TO CONSCIENCE and free profession, practice and propagation of religion (articles 25 to 28);

(v) The RIGHT OF MINORITIES to conserve their culture, language and script and to establish and administer educational institutions of their choice (articles 29 and 30); and

(vi) The RIGHT TO CONSTITUTIONAL REMEDIES for the enforcement of all these Fundamental Rights (article 32).

Some of the fundamental rights like 'equality before law' and 'equal protection of laws' (article 14), protection in respect of conviction for offences (article 20), protection of life and personal liberty (article 21) protection against arrest and detention in certain cases (article 22), freedom of religion (articles 25-28), etc. are avaiable to all 'persons'. There are, however, some rights which can be claimed only by the citizens, e.g. right not to be discriminated on grounds of religion, race, caste, sex or place of birth (article 15), equality of opportunity in the matter of public employment (article 16), and freedom of speech and exppression and association, movement, residence and profession (article 19).

Originally, article 19(1)(f) and article 31 contained the RIGHT TO PROPERTY, i.e. to acquire, hold and dispose off property subject to the right of the State to compulsory acquisition for public purpose by authority of law. However, the right to property ceased to be a fundamental right when the Constitution Forty-fourth Amendment Act, 1978 omitted sub-clause(f) of clause (1) of article 19 and the whole of article 31 from the Constitution.

Articles 31A and 31B inserted by the First Constitutional Amendment and article 31C inserted by the Twenty-fifth Amendment sought to protect laws providing for acquisition of estates, Acts and regulations specified in the Ninth Schedule, giving effect to Directive Principles.

Articles 33 to 35 deal with the power of Parliament to modify the rights conferred by Part III of the Constitution in their application to forces.

It is true that the fundamental human rights enshrined in the Constitution of India are hedged in by many limitations and restrictions. Replying to criticism that Fundamental Rights were riddled with so many restrictions that no value could be attached to them, and referring in particular to critics who had relied on the U.S. Constitution in support of their contention that Fundamental Rights were not 'fundamental' unless they were also 'absolute', Dr. Ambedkar observed in the Constituent Assembly on 4 November, 1948 as follows:

> "The whole of the criticism about fundamental rights is based upon a misconception. In the first place, the criticism insofar as it seeks to distinguish Fundamental rights from non-fundamental rights is not sound. It is incorrect to say that fundamental rights are absolute while non-fundamental rights are not absolute. The real distinction between the two is that non-fundamental rights are created by agreement between parties while fundamental rights are the gift of law. Because fundamental rights are the gift of the State it does not follow that the State cannot qualify them. In the second place, it is wrong to say that fundamental rights in America are absolute...The Supreme Court invented the doctrine of police power and refuted the advocates of absolute fundamental rights by the argument that every State has inherent in it police power which is not required to be conferred on it expressly by the Constitution... There is really no difference in the result. What one does it directly, the other does I indirectly. In both cases, the fundamental rights are not absolute."

The fundamental rights secured to the individual are in the nature of limitations or restrictions on the actions of the State. As Chief Justice Patanjali Sastry said:

> "The whole object of Part III of the Constitution is to provide protection for the freedoms and rights mentioned

therein against arbitrary invasion by the State.' (State of West Bengal v. Subodh Gopal Bose, AIR 1954 SC 92)."

Described by Dr. S. Radhakrishnan 'as a pledge to our people and a pact with the civilised world', the fundamental rights are made binding on the State, i.e. the Executive as well as the Legislature. Article 13(2) declares all laws and executive orders in force immediately before the commencement of the Constitution, in consistent with the fundamental rights to be ultra vires and void to the extent of such inconsistency. It also says:

> "The State shall not make any law which takes away or abridges the rights conferred by this part and any law made in contravention of this clause shall to the extent of contravention be void."

The article thus provides for judicial review of all legislation in India whether past or present though acts done before the commencement of the Constitution in contravention of the provisions of any law which becomes void by virtue of Part Ill, are not affected retrospectively. (Habeeb Mohd. v. State of Hyderabad, AIR 1953 SC 287).

In R. C. Cooper v Union of India (AIR 1973 SC 106), the Supreme Court expressed the view that the State action must be adjudged in the light of its operation upon the rights of the individual and group of individuals in all its dimensions Clause (4) of article 13.

Thanks makes it clear that the term "law" in that article does not cover constitutional amendments made under Article 368 and therefore the validity of a Constitutional Amendment cannot be questioned on the ground of its being violative of fundamental rights unless a fundamental right is held to be part of some Basic Feature of the Constitution. The National Commission to Review the Working of the Constitution, among others, recommended that:

(i) freedom of the press should be specifically mentioned as a fundamental right,

(ii) truth should be made admissible as a defence in CONTEMPT OF COURT cases,

(iii) those deprived of life or liberty should have an enforceable right to compensation,

(iv) law must ensure the right to rural wage employment for a minimum of 80 days in a year,

(v) right of access to Courts and Tribunals should be guaranteed to everyone and should include the right to reasonably speedy and effective equal justice and free legal aid should become fundamental rights,

(vi) every child should have the right to care and assistance and the right of free education up to 14 years of age, and

(vii) everyone should be guaranteed safe drinking water, protection of environment, prevention of pollution and ecological degradation, promotion of conservation, use of natural resources, etc.

Directive Principles

Directive Principles of State Policy are a unique feature of India's Constitution. These principles are embodied in Part IV, Articles 36 to 51. Inspired by the Irish Constitution of 1937, the Directive Principles are distinguished from Fundamental Rights by not being judicially enforceable but Directive Principles are not intended to be merely moral precepts but should be treated both, as positive mandates and a part and parcel of the human rights provisions of the Constitution. Directive Principles are described in Article 37 as being 'fundamental in the governance of the country' and which it shall be the duty of the State to apply in making laws.

Decisions of the Supreme Court from the 1970s onwards have emphasized the positive aspects of Directive Principles and treated them as supplements to Fundamental Rights for achieving the objective of social justice and a welfare State and for putting an end to economic exploitation and staggering inequalities and inequities.

Article 38 lays down that the State shall strive to promote the welfare of the people by securing and protecting a social order with social, economic and political justice. Article 39 ordains the State to strive to provide equally to men and women adequate means of livelihood, distribution of ownership and control of material resources to subserve common good, an economic system not resulting in concentration of wealth to common detriment, equal pay for equal work for men and women. Protection of health of workers and children and all citizens, opportunities to children to grow in healthy environment and protection of childhood and youth against exploitation, etc.

Article 39A asks the State to secure equal justice and free legal aid. Articles 40 to 45 provide for organization of village panchayats, provision for just and humane conditions of work and maternity leave, living wage, etc. for workers, workers' participation in management, and uniform civil code.

Articles 46 to 51 enjoin the State to provide early childhood care and education to children before the age of six, to promote the educational and economic interests of the Scheduled Castes and Scheduled Tribes, to raise the level of nutrition, standard of living and public health, to organize agriculture and animal husbandry, to protect environment, forests arid wild-life, to protect monuments, etc.. to take steps for separation of executive from the judiciary and to work for promotion of world peace and security.

Speaking in the Constituent Assembly, Dr. Ambedkar had categorically said that the Directive principles were not intended to be mere pious declarations. They were instead in the nature of an instrument of instructions and whoever captured power 'will have to respect these'. He had said:

> "It is the intention of the Assembly that in future both the legislature and the executive should not merely pay lip-service to these principles enacted in this part, but that they should be made the basis of all executive and legislative action that may be taken hereafter in the matter of the governance of the country."

8

Fundamental Duties of Every Citizen

When Gandhiji was requested to give his thoughts on the Universal Declaration of Human Rights, he said:

> "The source of right is duty. If we all discharge our duties, rights will not be far to seek. If leaving duties unperformed we run after rights, they will escape us like will-o'-the-wisp—the more we pursue them, the further they will fly."

I learned from my illiterate but wise mother that all rights to be deserved and preserved come from duty well done. Thus, the very right to live accrues to us only when we do the duty of citizenship of the world. From this one fundamental statement, perhaps it is easy enough to define duties of man and woman and correlate every right to some corresponding duty to be first performed. Every other right can be shown to be a usurpation hardly worth fighting for.

There can be no rights in a society where there are no duties. Rights and duties are not only reconcilable but inseparable. For every right, there is a corresponding duty. Duty is an inalienable part of right; the two represent the two sides of the same coin. What is duty for one is another's right and vice versa. If all men have a right to life, a duty is also cast upon all men to respect human life and not to injure another person. The right to freedom implies that the citizens must create conditions so that freedom for every individual is assured. Freedom requires self-discipline and promotion of social and political harmony. For, the freedom of one individual is limited by the similar freedom of other individuals and each individual has a duty to accord the same rights to others which he wants for himself. Freedom for each individual can endure when one respects the freedom of all other individuals. Discharge of duties by them strengthens their own rights.

The Constitution (42nd Amendment) Act, 1976, added a new Part IV-A (Article 51A) containing a charter of Fundamental Duties for citizens. It was a thought appropriate that citizenship must carry with it certain fundamental obligations and that these should be specifically and explicitly be incorporated in the Constitution. The Fundamental Duties chapter is now one of the most valuable parts of the Constitution. As the Verma Committee (Ministry of Human Resource Development, Government of India, 1999) on Fundamental Duties said:

> "Essentially all that is contained in the Fundamental Duties is just a codification of tasks integral to the Indian way of life...it would be essential to create public awareness of the need to appreciate and internalise the concept and practice of Fundamental Duties—with particular emphasis on the necessity of creating a harmonious society with a scientific outlook, free from tensions and turmoils."

The Supreme Court of India has in several cases relied on Fundamental Duties contained in Article 5 I A to determine the duty of the State. The new Part IVA, article 51A (a) to (k) lays down eleven duties for every citizen of India:

1. To abide by the Constitution and respect its ideals and institutions, the National Flag and the National Anthem.
2. To cherish and follow the noble ideals which inspired India's national struggle for freedom.
3. To uphold and protect the Sovereignty, and Unity and Integrity of India.
4. To defend the country and render national service when called upon to do so. Here, mention may be made of article 23(2) whereunder the State is allowed to impose 'compulsory service for public purposes' subject to the condition that no discrimination is made on grounds of religion, race, caste or class or any of them.
5. To promote harmony and the spirit of common brotherhood amongst all the people of India transcending religious, linguistic and regional or sectional diversities; to renounce practices derogatory to the dignity of women.
6. To value and preserve the rich heritage of India's composite culture.
7. To protect and improve the natural environment including forests, lakes, rivers and wild life, and to have compassion for living creatures.
8. To develop the scientific temper, humanism and the spirit of inquiry and reform.
9. To safeguard public property and to abjure violence.
10. To strive towards excellence in all spheres of individual and collective activity, so that the nation constantly rises to higher levels of endeavour and achievement.
11. Every parent or guardian to provide opportunities for education to his child or ward between the age of 6 and 14 years.

There is no provision in the Constitution for direct enforcement of the Fundamental Duties enshrined in article 5 1 A, nor is there any provision to prevent or punish their violation. But, as Justice Venaktaramiah has pointed out, there is no provision declaring them non-justiciable either and in the context of use of words like 'fundamental' and 'duties', these should *prima facie* be enforceable. It may be expected that in determining the constitutionality of any law, if Supreme Court finds that it seeks to give effect to any of these duties, it may consider such law to be 'reasonable' in relation to article 14 or 19 and thus save such law from unconstitutionality [Mohan V. Union of India, (1992) 1 SCC 594]. The purpose of incorporating the Fundamental Duties in the Constitution is to make citizens aware of their social and economic obligations and to warn them to do and not to do certain things in the interest of their country, their fellow citizens and themselves.

For the implementation of at least some of the fundamental duties of citizens, as the Verma Committee (1999) stated, legal provisions exist:

A. The Emblems and Names (Prevention of Improper Use) Act 1950 was enacted soon after independence, *inter alia*, to prevent improper use of the National Flag and the National Anthem.

B. In order to ensure that no disrespect is shown to the National Flag, Constitution of India and the National Anthem, the Prevention of Insults to National Honour Act 1971 was enacted.

C. In order to ensure that correct usage regarding display of the National Flag is well understood, the instructions issued from time to time on the subject have been embodied in Flag Code India which has been made available to all the State Governments and Union Territory Administrations (UTs).

D. There are a number of provisions in the existing criminal laws to ensure that the activities which encourage enmity between different groups of people grounds of religion, race, place of birth, residence, language, etc. are adequately punished. Writings, speeches, gestures, activities, exercises, drills, etc. aimed at creating a feeling of insecurity or ill-will among the members of other communities, etc. have been prohibited under Section 153A of the Indian Penal Code (IPC).

E. Imputations and assertions prejudicial to nation are made a punishable offence under Section 153B of IPC.

F. Communal organisations can be declared unlawful association under the provisions of Unlawful Activities (Prevention) Act 1967. Offences related to religion and caste are covered in Sections 295 to 298 of the IPC and provisions of the Protection of Civil Rights Act, I 955 (earlier the Untouchability (Offences) Act 1955). Section 123(3) and (3A) of the Representation of People Act, 1951, declare that soliciting of votes on the ground of religion and the promotion or attempt to promote feelings of enmity or hatred between different classes of citizens of India on grounds of religion, race, caste, community or language is a corrupt practice. A person indulging in a corrupt practice can be disqualified for being a Member of Parliament or a State Legislature under Section 8A of the Representation of People Act.

The courts can take fundamental duties of citizens into consideration while construing a law amenable to more than one interpretation.

Article 5 1 A(g) regarding protection of environment has particularly come up before the courts. Oral orders were issued by the Supreme Court for stopping quarrying operations in some areas in the State of UP. Also, orders were issued in respect of declaring certain disputed areas as reserved forests under the Indian Forests Act 1927.

The rulers and the legislators—the ministers, the lawmakers and the administrators—have to be conscious not only of the fundamental duties of citizens at large but also of their own fundamental duties as citizens. It is one of their most fundamental constitutional obligations to be all the time aware of the Fundamental Rights of the citizens under the Constitution. For, wherever an obligation is cast on the 'State', it is for the citizens in positions of authority to implement it.

A good citizen is law abiding. Enlightened citizenship requires placing public interest above personal interest. Individual citizens should observe certain standards of self-discipline, respect the rights of others, perform their duties to society, and train themselves in the art of peaceful living and democratic governance through implementation of their Fundamental Rights and Citizenship Duties. Only with such a responsible citizenry can both the individual citizen and the society develop to their full potential and democratic polity attain its full stature.

The 11 Fundamental Constitutional Duties for citizens are morally and ethically binding on all of us. In addition, every Article of the Constitution casts a duty on citizens to see it fulfilled in letter and spirit.

9

Structure of Indian Polity

The Union Executive and Legislature

India very consciously chose for itself the system of parliamentary democracy with ministerial responsibility to the representatives of the people elected by universal adult franchise. But it would be wrong to assume that it was the British parliamentary system. A mix of the parliamentary and presidential systems, it was India's own model as it gradually evolved through the nationalist struggle for freedom with responsive and responsible self-rule and finally through deliberations of the Constituent Assembly.

India is not a small, unitary, island state nor is it a monarchy like the UK. India is a large republic and a Union of States, like the United States, with an elected President as the head of the Republic. With distribution of powers between the Union and the States, the Constitution also establishes a semblance of federal polity. India is thus in the unique position of being at once a parliamentary polity and a republic with a sort of federal structure. While India is a 'Union of States', it is an indestructible and indissoluble union. The units have no power of secession. Unlike the UK again, India has a written Constitution which establishes three main organs of the State—the Executive, the Legislature and the Judiciary— and defines their respective jurisdictions and *inter se* relationships. All executive powers of the Union is vested in the President. The President has:

1. Executive powers to be exercised by him directly or through officers;
2. Powers to appoint high functionaries of the State including the Prime Minister, other Ministers, Governors, Judges of the Supreme Court and the various High Courts;
3. Military powers as the Supreme Commander of the armed forces with the authority to declare war and peace;
4. Power to grant pardon, reprieve, etc.;
5. Diplomatic powers, including appointment of ambassadors and receiving credentials of foreign diplomatic representatives;
6. Legislative powers including powers to summon and prorogue Houses and dissolve Lok Sabha, give assent to Bills, etc. and issue ordinances having the force of law; and
7. Emergency powers.

Despite all this array of impressive powers, the Indian President's position is conceived as that of a constitutional head of State. Article 74(1) requires the President to act only with the aid and advice of the Council of Ministers in the discharge of all his functions. This follows also from India's adoption of the parliamentary form of government with ministerial responsibility.

India's President is elected for five years by an electoral college consisting of the elected members of the two houses of Parliament and the legislative assemblies of the states by a system of proportional representation with single transferable vote. The President can be removed by the two houses of Parliament by impeachment for violation of the Constitution.

The Vice-President is elected by members of the two houses of Parliament and is the *ex officio* Chairman of Rajya Sabha.

The Prime Minister is appointed by the President, and the other Ministers are appointed by him on the advice of the Prime Minister. The Ministers hold office during the pleasure of the President. The Council of Ministers is collectively responsible to the Lok Sabha. Therefore, it stands or falls together. If it loses the confidence of the House, the entire Council of Ministers must resign. Also, collective responsibility mean that the Ministers must not speak in public in different voices.

The Parliament of the Union consists of the President and the two Houses. Thus, the President is a constituent part of Parliament. On the advice of the Council of Ministers, he summons and prorogues the two Houses and can dissolve Lok Sabha. All bills need his assent to become law.

Rajya Sabha, or the Council of States, is really conceived as a house of the States. It is elected by members of the Legislative Assemblies of the various states. The term of each member is six years. One-third of the total number of members retire every two years. It is thus a continuous house and is not subject to dissolution. Twelve members are nominated by the President. The maximum number of members can be 250.

Lok Sabha is the House of the People and its members are elected directly by the people from territorial constituencies. Up to two members may be nominated by the President to represent the Anglo-Indian community. The maximum number of members can be 552. Seats are reserved for the Scheduled Castes and the Scheduled Tribes. The term of the House is five years. While the two houses are equal in status, the Lok Sabha has special powers in regard to money bills and no-confidence motions.

The Executive in India is a part of the Parliament, comes from it, remains a part of it, and is responsible to its popular House, the Lok Sabha. There is thus a fusion of the highest executive and legislative authorities in parliamentary polity. Dr. Ambedkar noted in the Constituent Assembly:

> "A democratic executive must satisfy two conditions— (1) It must be a stable executive, and (2) it must be a responsible executive. Unfortunately, it has not been possible so far to devise a system which can ensure both in equal degree. You can have a system which can give you more stability but less responsibility or you can have a system which gives you more responsibility but less stability. The American and the Swiss systems give more stability but less responsibility. The British System on the other hand gives you more responsibility but less stability…The Draft Constitution in recommending the Parliamentary system of Executive has preferred more responsibility to more stability."

Council of Ministers

Article 74 of the Constitution lays down that there shall be a Council of Ministers with the Prime Minister at the head to aid and advise the President who shall, in the exercise of his functions, act in accordance with such advice. The President may, however, require the Council of Ministers to reconsider such advice. The President shall act on the advice tendered after such reconsideration.

That there shall be a Council of Ministers has to be understood to mean that it shall always be there. The Constitution does not envisage a situation where there will be no Prime Minister or no Council of Ministers. There is no provision for failure of constitutional machinery (as under article 356) and direct President's Rule at the Union level.

Acceptance by the President of the advice tendered by the Council of Ministers has become obligatory particularly after the 42nd and 44th Constitutional Amendments. Even before those amendments the Supreme Court had taken the view that the advice was binding in all cases (Samsher v. State of Punjab, AIR 1974 SC 2192).

Even after the dissolution of Lok Sabha, the President, in the exercise of his powers, was bound by the aid and advice of the Council of Ministers. It was held by the Supreme Court in U. N. Rao v. Indira Gandhi (AIR 1971 SC 1002) that any exercise of powers by the President without the advice of the Council of Ministers shall be unconstitutional as being violative of article 74(1).

However, the acceptance of the advice of the Council of Ministers by the President is not automatic or mechanical. The President is entitled to consider it by applying his mind. The 44th Amendment allows to the President an opportunity to advise and caution the Council of Ministers and seek reconsideration of any matter before the President puts his seal of approval and accepts the proposed course of action.

Under article 75, the Prime Minister is appointed by the President. Other Ministers are appointed by him on the advice of the Prime Minister and hold office during the pleasure of the President. The Council of Ministers is collectively responsible to Lok Sabha.

While the President is to be fully guided in the discharge of all his functions by the advice of the Council of Ministers with the Prime Minister at its head, it is not clear as to on whose advice he performs the most crucial function of appointing the Prime Minister. So far as the letter of the Constitution goes, the President can appoint almost anyone as the Prime

Minister but he has to remember that under the Constitution the Council of Ministers headed by the Prime Minister has to be responsible to the House and would have to go if it loses the confidence of the Lok Sabha. The President, therefore would appoint only a person who, in his best judgement would be acceptable to the House. If a party or a pre-election alliance commands absolute majority support in the Lok Sabha, there is no difficulty. For, the President in such cases, following well established parliamentary practices and conventions, has to invite the Leader of the majority party, front or alliance to take over as the Prime Minister and form a Government., But, where no single party or coalition is in a position to form a Government on its own, the role of the President in choosing the Prime Minister becomes most delicate and difficult. He may have to use all his abilities to decide on the leader most likely to command the confidence of Lok Sabha. He may call the leader of the single largest party or alliance first or seek to be satisfied in advance about a leader having the support of more than half of the members of the Lok Sabha.

10

Judiciary

Supreme Court

Even though Judiciary under the Constitution of India is one integrated hierarchy of courts—from the subordinate courts to the Supreme Court of India and we do not have the system of separate courts for administering the Union and State laws, the Supreme Court of India is mentioned under the head 'Union Judiciary' (articles 124 to 147). High Courts and Subordinate Courts are covered under articles 214 to 237.

India's Supreme Court came into being on 28 January 1950. The inauguration took place in the old Chamber of Princes in the Parliament building. It was, in this Chamber of Princes, that the Federal Court of India had sat for 12 years between 1937 and 1950. This was to be the home of the Supreme Court for years that were to follow until the Supreme Court acquired its own present premises in 1958.

The original Constitution of 1950 under article 124 envisaged a Supreme Court with a Chief and 7 puisne Judges—leaving it to Parliament to increase this number. In the early years, all the Judges of the Supreme Court sat together to hear the cases presented before them. As the work of the Court increased and arrears of cases began to accumulate, Parliament increased the number of Judges from 8 in 1950 to 11 in 1956, 14 in 1960, 18 in 1978 and 26 in 1986, including the Chief Justice. As at the end of 2021, it was 34. As the number of the judges has increased, they sit in smaller benches of two and three — coming together in larger benches of 5 and more only when required to do so or to settle a difference of opinion or controversy.

In order to be appointed as a Judge of the Supreme Court, a person must be a citizen of India and must have been, for at least five years, a Judge of a High Court or of two or more such Courts in succession, or an Advocate of a High Court or of two or more such Courts in succession for at least 10 years or he must be, in the opinion of the President, a distinguished jurist [article 124(3)]. Supreme Court Judges retire upon attaining the age of 65 years. A judge may be removed from his office only by an order of the President passed after an address passed by each House of Parliament for his removal 'on the ground of misbehavior or incapacity' supported by a majority of the total membership of that House and by a majority of not less than two-thirds of the members present and voting is presented to him in the same session. The procedure may be regulated by Parliament by law [articles 124(2), (4) & (5)]. Before he enters upon his office, every person appointed as a judge of the Supreme Court takes an oath before the President or some person appointed in that behalf by him in the form prescribed in the Constitution. The Constitution prohibits a person who has held office as a judge of the Supreme Court from practising law before any court in the territory of India [articles 124(6) & (7)]. When the office of the Chief Justice is vacant, or when the Chief Justice is unable to perform the duties of his office due to absence, the President shall appoint an Acting Chief Justice from among the judges of the Court to perform the duties of the Chief Justice (article 126).

The Chief Justice of India may invite a retired judge of the Supreme Court or a retired judge of the High Court having the qualification to be a judge of the Supreme Court, to sit and act as a judge of the Supreme Court for such period as he deems necessary. This can be done with the previous consent of the President, and also of the person to be so appointed (article 128).

Under article 142 of the Constitution 'The Supreme Court in the exercise of its jurisdiction may pass such decree or make such order as is necessary for doing complete justice in any cause or matter pending before it.'

The exclusive original jurisdiction of the Supreme Court extends to any dispute between the Government of India and one or more States, or between the Government of India and any State or States on one side and one or more States on the other or between two or more States, if and insofar as the dispute involves any question (whether of law or of fact) on which the existence or extent of a legal right de-pends (article 131).

The original jurisdiction of the Supreme Court also extends to cases of violation of the Fundamental Rights of individuals and the Court can issue several writs for the enforcement of these rights (article 32). It is empowered to issue directions, orders or writs, including writs in the nature of *Habeas Corpus, Mandamus, Prohibition, Quo Warranto* and *Certiorari* to enforce them. It is a unique feature of India's Constitution that in principle, any individual can straight-away approach the highest court in case of violation of his fundamental rights.

Under article 139A inserted by the 44th Amendment in 1978, the Supreme Court may transfer to itself cases from one or more High Courts if these involve questions of law or of great importance. Also, the Supreme Court may transfer cases from one High Court to another in the interests of justice.

The Supreme Court, if satisfied that cases involving the same or substantially the same questions of law are pending before it and one or more High Courts or before two or more High Courts and that such questions are substantial questions of general importance, may withdraw a case or cases pending before the High Court or High Courts and dispose of all such cases itself.

Under article 138, the Supreme Court shall have such further jurisdiction and powers with respect to any of the matters in the Union List as Parliament may by law confer. It shall have such jurisdiction and powers with respect to any matter as the Government of India and the Government of any state may by special agreement confer, if the Parliament by law provides for the exercise of such jurisdiction and powers by the Supreme Court. This enlarges the jurisdiction of the Supreme Court and provides it with very special jurisdiction to hear cases of most urgent nature directly and in its original jurisdiction for speedy disposal.

Article 139 lays down that Parliament may by law confer on the Supreme Court power to issue directions, orders or writs in matters not already covered under article 32. Under article 140, Parliament may by law supplement the powers of the Supreme Court. Law declared by the Supreme Court is binding on all courts in India vide article 141.

Decrees and orders of the Supreme Court shall be enforceable throughout India and civil and judicial authorities shall act in aid of the Supreme Court (articles 142 and 144). For purposes of giving effect to the directions and decisions of the Supreme Court, all authorities, civil and judicial, in the territory of India, have been made subordinate to the authority of the Supreme Court in as much as all these are required to 'act in aid of the Supreme Court' (article 144). The Supreme Court may from time to time, and with the approval of the

President, make rules for regulating generally the practice and procedure of the Court.

The officers and staff of the Supreme Court are appointed by the Chief Justice of India, by such other judge or officer of the court as he may direct (articles 145-146).

Under article 124 (2), the Supreme Court judges were to be appointed by the President 'after consultation with such of the judges of the Supreme Court and the High Courts' as the President may deem necessary. The proviso to the article said that 'in the case of appointment of a judge other than the Chief justice, the Chief justice of India shall always be consulted.' In the S.P. Gupta v. Union of India case, the court held that the consultation must be effective and involve exchange of views and examination of merits but it did not mean concurrence and ultimately the executive had the last word in the matter inasmuch as the power of appointment vested in the President as advised by the Council of Ministers. The question was considered by a nine-judge Bench in Supreme Court Advocates on-Record Association v. Union of India, (1993). Justice Verma, delivering the majority judgment, stressed the constitutional purpose of selecting best available persons as judges. The result of the landmark judgment was that the Chief Justice, in consultation with other senior judges was supposed to be in the best position to decide upon the best person to don the Bench. Thus the Supreme Court practically took over the power of the appointment of Judges in its own hands, notwithstanding the clear words in article 124(2) of the Constitution.

The procedure for appointment was revised in the light of this judgment in 1994 to the effect that the decisive view in the matter of the appointment of judges shall be that of the Chief Justice of India and in a case of a vacancy in the office of the Chief Justice of India, the senior most judge shall be appointed, unless the retiring Chief reported that he was unfit. But, then in the Constituent Assembly, Dr. Ambedkar had said: "...after all, the Chief Justice is a man with all the failings, all the sentiments and all the prejudices which we as common people have; and I think, to allow the Chief Justice practically a veto upon the appointment of judges is really to transfer the authority to the Chief Justice which we are not prepared to vest in the President or the Government of the day... This is a dangerous proposition". Also, according to one former CJI (Justice ES Venkataramaiah), in the interpretation placed by the majority of judges on article 124, the

> "text of the Constitution seems to have been departed from…The interpretation now given neutralizes the position of the President and makes article 74 which requires the President to act on the aid and advice of the Council of Ministers irrelevant. The construction now placed by the court makes the Supreme Court and the High Courts totally undemocratic. While in a parliamentary democracy the President may be a mere constitutional head when the power is exercised by him on the advice of the Council of Ministers, he cannot be asked to play the same limited role where the Chief Justice of India who is not an elected representative advises him. One cannot ignore that this may lead on a future occasion to tyranny in another unexpected place... The new meaning given by the Supreme Court appears to be beyond the scope of mere interpretation and virtually amounts to rewriting the relevant constitutional provision".

The position as it emerged after the Ninety-ninth Constitution Amendment and the National Judicial Appointment Commission Act was that the collegium system under which during the last twenty years the judges themselves, selected the judges had been given a good bye and replaced by the National Judicial Appointments Commission (NJAC)—a body consisting of the Chief Justice of India (Chairman), Union Minister of Law and Justice, two senior-most judges of the Supreme Court and two 'eminent person' nominated by the Prime Minister, CJI and the leader of the largest party in opposition in the Lok Sabha. The constitutionality of the proposed NJAC was successfully challenged. Constitution Bench of the Supreme Court declared it ultra vires the Constitution. However, for anything to be declared unconstitutional, the point of reference has to be the Constitution itself. We must go by what the Constitution says, on that basis, the judgment of the Supreme Court in the NJAC case may itself seem unconstitutional.

Even the Supreme Court is not above the Constitution. The constituent I, power vested in Parliament cannot be transferred to itself by the Supreme Court. As has been stated elsewhere, to paraphrase differently Supreme Court's own observations in the Minerva Mills case about Parliament's amending powers, one is tempted to say:

Since 'the Constitution had conferred a limited' power of judicial review and of interpreting the Constitution only for 'doing complete justice' within its 'jurisdiction', the Supreme Court cannot 'under the exercise of that limited power enlarge that very power into an absolute power'. Indeed, limited judicial review 'is one of the basic features of our Constitution and, therefore, the limitations on that power cannot be destroyed'. In other words, the Supreme Court, under articles 32, 141 and 142 cannot expand its power of interpretation so as to acquire for itself the right to amend or prevent amendment to the Constitution on the ground of a self-invented 'basic features' doctrine or thereby in effect destroy the most basic feature of Indian polity, namely the primacy of the people and democracy as a Government of the people, by the people and for the people. It is the people and the Constitution framed by their representatives that have given certain limited powers to the Supreme Court as to other organs. 'The donee of a limited power cannot by exercise of that power convert the limited power into an unlimited one'. The problem remains unresolved for students of the Constitution.

The Removal of Judges

A judge of the Supreme Court or any High Court can be removed from his office by the President, only if a joint address passed by both Houses of Parliament with a special majority (i.e., by a majority of the total membership of the Houses and by a majority of not less than two-thirds of the members of each House present and voting) is presented to him (article 124(4) and 218).

Parliament is not empowered to discuss the conduct of any judge of the Supreme Court or of a High Court in the discharge of his duties except in the case of a motion for presenting an address to the President praying for the removal of a Judge (article 121).

Contrary to the common belief, there is no provision in our Constitution for the impeachment of a judge. The impeachment is provided only for the President. Also, there is a fundamental difference between removal procedure and impeachment procedure and between the impact of the adoption of a motion for impeachment and the passing of a motion for presenting an address to the President seeking orders for the removal of a judge. The majority required for impeachment of the President is different. Also the grounds for the impeachment of the President have to concern 'violation of the Constitution' while an address for removal of a judge has to be on the ground of 'misbehavior or incapacity'. In case of impeachment, the moment the motion is passed by the two Houses, the President forthwith ceases to be the President. But in case of the motion for removal, it is for the President to consider issuing necessary orders.

High Courts

The Constitution provides for a High Court for each State. Parliament may, however establish by law a common High Court for two or more States or for two or more States and a Union territory (articles 214 and 231). Among the Union Territories only J&K and Delhi a High Court. Other Union Territories come under the jurisdiction of different State High Courts.

Each High Court comprises of a Chief Justice and such other Judges as the President may, from time to time, appoint (article 216). Judges of the High Court are appointed by the President after consultation with the Chief Justice of India, the Governor of the State and in case of appointment of all judges other than the Chief Justice, the Chief Justice of the High Court.

To be appointed a High Court judge, a person must be a citizen of India with ten years' service in a judicial office or ten years' experience as a High Court advocate. On appointment, every High Court judge must take an oath of office. Every High Court judge shall hold office until he attains the age of 62. He cannot be removed from his office except in the manner provided for removal of a judge of the Supreme Court. Further, to ensure the independence of the office of a High Court judge, it is laid down that after being a permanent judge of a High Court, a person shall not plead in any court in India except the Supreme Court or other High Courts. Every

High Court judge is entitled to a salary and allowances as may be settled by Parliament by law or as specified in the Second Schedule to the Constitution.

Judges may be transferred from one High Court to another by the President after consulting the Chief Justice of India (article 222). However, the Supreme Court has held that Judicial Review is necessary to check arbitrariness and that a High Court judge cannot be transferred without his consent but that only the judge affected can question it. [Union of India v. Sankal Chand, AIR 1977 SC 2328; K. Ashok Reddy v. Govt of India, JT (1994) 1 S C 40]. The President may appoint an acting Chief Justice for a High Court. Also, in case of need, the President may appoint additional and acting judges of the High Court for a period not exceeding two years. The Chief Justice of a High Court may, with the consent of the President, appoint a retired judge to sit and act as a judge (articles 215, 217-224A).

Every High Court has full control over its staff. The salaries and allowances of the judges and of the High Court staff are all charged on the Consolidated Fund of the State. Appointments of officers and staff of a High Court are made by the Chief Justice of the Court or by such other judge or officer of the Court as he may decide. The terms and conditions of service of the staff and officers of the Court should appropriately be settled by rules made by the Chief Justice and approved by the President (article 229). The jurisdiction of a High Court may be extended to or excluded from a Union territory (article 230).

Article 226 lays down that every High Court shall have power throughout the territory under its jurisdiction to issue to any person or authority directions, orders or writs including writs of *Habeas Corpus,* Prohibition, *Quo Warranto* and *Certiorari* or any of them for the enforcement of the fundamental rights or for any other purpose. Thus, while the Supreme Court's writ jurisdiction extends only to cases of violation of fundamental rights, the High Courts under article 226 enjoy much wider powers and can issue writs in all cases of breach of any right. This becomes obvious from the use of the term 'for any other purpose'. The High Court may set aside an illegal, order, may declare the law or the right, may order relief by way of, for example, refund of illegal tax, etc. Just as the law declared by the Supreme Court is binding on all courts in India, that declared by the High Court is binding on all subordinate courts within the State or within the territory covered by the jurisdiction of the High Court.

It needs to be remembered that the remedy through a writ in cases other than those of violation of Fundamental Rights is not a normal one and is not expected to be granted as a matter of routine. It is an extraordinary remedy which can be expected in special circumstances and only under the discretion of the Court. Judiciary is not supposed to lay down policy and no court or tribunal can compel the government to change its policy involving expenditure. [Himmat Lal Shah v. State of UP, AIR 1954 SC 403; Abraham v. ITO, AIR 1961 SC 609; Bhopal Sugar Industry v. ITO, AIR 1967 SC 549; State of Rajasthan v. Karam Chand, AIR 1965 SC 913; Union of India v. Tejram, (991) 3 SCC 11; Kartar Singh v. State of Punjab, JT (1994) 2 SC 423] where any High Court is satisfied that a case pending in the lower courts involves a substantial question of law as to the interpretation of the Constitution, it may withdraw the case and either itself decide it or determine the said question of law and return the case to the lower Court for determination (article 228).

Like the Supreme Court, each High Court is also to be a Court of record and of original and appellate jurisdiction with all the powers of such a court including the power to punish for its contempt (article 215).

Subordinate Courts

Subordinate courts, at the level of districts and lower, have almost similar structure all over the country. They deal with civil and criminal cases in accordance with their respective jurisdictions and administer the Code of Civil Procedure and the Code of Criminal Procedure. Each state is divided into judicial districts. The subordinate Judiciary in each district is headed by a District and Sessions Judge. The usual designations on the civil side are District Judge, Additional District Judge, Civil Judge. On the criminal side, there are Sessions Judge, Additional Sessions Judge, Chief Judicial Magistrate, Judicial Magistrate, etc. The Governor in consultation with the High Court appoints the district judges. A person who is not already in government service should have at least seven years' experience at the bar to become eligible for the position of a district judge (article 233).

Appointment of persons other than district judges to the judicial service of a state shall be made by the Governor in accordance with rules made thereunder. Besides the State Public Service Commission, the High Court has to be consulted in the matter of such appointments (article 234).

The administrative control of the High Court over the district courts and other lower courts is full inasmuch as posting, promotions and grant of leave, etc to any person belonging to the judicial service of a state and holding any post inferior to the post of a judge is vested in the High Court (article 235).

11

State Executive and Legislature

State Executive

As we have seen in chapter 5, India is a Union of States and its territory is now divided between 28 States and 8 Union Territories. So far as the structure and functions of the main organs of the State are concerned, these are, generally speaking, very similar to those at the Union level. True to the parliamentary model, there is a constitutional head called the Governor in whom the executive power of the State is vested. The one difference between the President of the Union and the Governor of a State is that while the President is the elected head of the Union, the Governor is appointed by the President and holds office during his (President's) pleasure. The real political executive is the Council of Ministers responsible to the directly elected representatives of the people in the Legislative Assembly of the State. The Governor is normally expected to act on the advice of his Council of Ministers 'except in so far as' he is required to function 'in his discretion'(article 163).

There are certain areas where the Governor may have to use his own wisdom and discretion, e.g. in (a) appointing a new Chief Minister in a situation where no single party or leader commands majority support; (b) dismissing a Ministry where it refuses to resign even after losing majority support in the House or after being defeated on a no-confidence motion; (c) dissolution of the Assembly on the advice of a Chief Minister who has lost majority support; (d) determining the royalty for mineral licenses to District Councils in case of tribal areas of Assam, under the Sixth Schedule; (e) advising the President of the failure of the constitutional machinery and to impose President's Rule; and (f) giving or withholding assent to Bills, returning a Bill for reconsideration of the House/s or reserving it for the consideration of the President. Some of the Governors may have to discharge certain special responsibilities also under Articles 371 to 371J.

There are a few 'special' provisions applicable to particular States: Gujarat and Maharashtra (article 371), Nagaland (article 371A), Assam (371B), Manipur (371C), Andhra Pradesh Telangana (371D), University in Andhra Pradesh (371E), Sikkim (article 371F), Mizoram (371G), Arunachal Pradesh (371H), Goa (371I) and Karnataka (371J).

Till recently (before 5 August, 2019), the State of Jammu & Kashmir was the only State which although an integral part of India, had a separate State Constitution of its own and all the provisions of the Constitution of India did not apply. Relations between the State of J & K and the Union of India were determined under article 370 of the Constitution of India. This article was, however, not described as a 'special' provision. It was specifically called a 'temporary' provision. Also, the article had an inbuilt procedure of self-erosion and extinction. In accordance with the article itself, on 5 August, 2019, a Presidential Order was issued whereby the 'temporary' status was ended and all the provisions of the Constitution of India were made applicable to J &K . By a separate Act, the

State of J&K was bifurcated and made the Union Territories of (1) J&K and (2) Ladakh.

State Legislature

The Legislature of a State consists of the Governor and the Legislative Assembly except that in some states there are two Houses—the Legislative Assembly and the Legislative Council. The term of the Assembly shall be five years. There be a continuing House not subject to dissolution but members shall retire every two years (article 172).

The House, or each house, of the State Legislature is from time to time summoned to meet by the Governor who may also prorogue the house or either house and dissolve the Legislative Assembly, The period for which the house/s should meet or the quired duration of the sessions is not laid down in the Constitution but the gap between two sessions must be less than six months (article 174).

Article 175 provides for the right of the Governor to address or send messages to the House or Houses of the State Legislature. Under article 176, the Governor is obliged to address the House or the Houses assembled together at the beginning of the first session each year and at the commencement of the first session after each general election to the Legislative Assembly of the State (176). All the Ministers and the Advocate General have a right to speak and take part in the proceeding of the house/s (article 177).

The State Legislature has exclusive jurisdiction to legislate on items in the State List and concurrent jurisdiction in respect of items in List III (articles 245-246). The position of the Legislative Council in a state is similar to that of the Rajya Sabha at the Uunion level. This applies *inter alia* to the privileges and immunities of legislatures, disqualification of members, relation between the two Houses, legislative procedure, origin of Money Bills, etc.

The assembly has a Speaker and a Deputy Speaker elected by the House and having the same position and functions as their Lok Sabha counterparts. The Council, however, also has a Chairman and Deputy Chairman elected by the Council (articles 178-187).

General rules for conduct of business in the Legislative Assembly/Council (articles 188 and 189), provisions regarding disqualification of members, vacating of seats, penalty for unauthorisedly sitting in the house (article 190-193), pawers, privileges and immunities for houses oi legislatures and members and committees (article 194), salaries and allowances of members (article 195), legislative procedure including that for passing money bills and other Bills (article 196-200 and 208-212), procedure in financial matters (article 202- 207) are all very similar to corresponding provisions in regard to the Union Parliament. Article 200 and 201 however, *inter alia* provide for the Governor reserving some bills for the consideration of the President and then the President assenting to the bills or withholding assent. Corresponding to the President's power under 123, the Governor also enjoys power to issue Ordinances (artic1e 213).

Union Territories

Union Territories are, by definition, directly Union administered. Article 239 *inter alia* provides that 'every Union Territory shall be administered by the President acting to such extent as he thinks fit, through an administrator to be appointed by him with such designation as he may specify.' The usual designation used is that of Lt. Governor. Also, Parliament may make laws for the administration of Union Territories. It may by a law created for any of these territories by a legislature and a Council of Ministers with limited powers in some areas. At present, these institutions exist for Puducherry, National Capital Territory of Delhi and J&K.

12

Union-State Relations

Part XI of the Constitution deals specifically with matters in the area of relations between the Union and the States. Chapter I of Part XI provides for distribution of Legislative Powers and Chapter II outlines administrative relations.

A great deal of damage has been caused as a result of the wrong use of the term 'Centre-State' instead of 'Union-State'. The Constitution does not use the term 'centre'; actually 'Central government', 'Central legislature', 'Central laws' etc. are an unfortunate hang-over from the days of a centralised government did the colonial rule, 'Centre' and 'Union' create very different images and connote concepts very different. 'Centre' is a point in the middle of the circle while 'Union' is the whole circle. The relationship between the Union and the States is that between the whole and the parts and not between the Centre of authority and its peripheries.

Legislative Relations Parliament may make laws for the whole or any part of India. The Legislature of a State may make laws for the whole or any part of the State. The Seventh Schedule to the Constitution embodies three lists, viz. the Union List, the State List and the Concurrent List consisting of 97, 66 and 47 items respectively. Article 246 lays down that the Union Parliament would have exclusive jurisdiction to make laws in regard to items in the Union List, the State Legislature would have exclusive power to make laws in respect of items in the State List and both the Union and State Legislatures could legislate in the area of items included in the Concurrent List. In case of any inconsistency between laws made by Parliament and those made by the Legislature of a State in respect of items in the Concurrent List, the Union law shall prevail and the State law shall be void to the extent of inconsistency except where a State law is reserved for the consideration of the President and receives his assent. Residuary powers of legislation have been left with the Union (Article 248). Also, Parliament has been given the power to make any law for the whole or any part of the country to give effect to any international treaty, agreement, convention or decision.

The Union List consists of subjects which are of common interest to the Union, and with respect to which, uniformity of legislation throughout the Union is essential. Subjects which allow for diversity of interest and treatment are included in the State List and matters in which uniformity of legislation throughout the Union is desirable but not essential are included in the Concurrent List.

Again, under article 250, Parliament is empowered to make laws on any item included in the State List for the whole or any part of India while a Proclamation of Emergency is in operation. The maximum duration of validity of such laws will be six months after the expiry of the Emergency.

In case of inconsistency between laws made by Parliament under articles 249 and 250 and laws made by State Legislatures, the law made by Parliament shall prevail and the State law shall be inoperative to the extent of repugnancy while the law made by Parliament remains in effect (article 25 1). Under the Doctrine of Pith and Substance, any jurisdictional conflict between the Union and the State/s in regard to their legislative competence can be settled by the Supreme Court ascertaining the substance of the matter relating to an item in one list or the other.

According to article 252, two or more State Legislatures by passing a resolution may ask Parliament to make laws on any matter in the State List. Such laws can be extended to other States provided the concerned State Legislatures pass resolutions to that effect.

Administrative Relations

Articles 256 to 265 seek to regulate administrative relations between the Union and the States. It is common in federal systems that the administrative relations between the Union and the States are fraught with difficulties. The Constitution of India seeks to achieve smooth working relationship between the two levels. It provides that the executive powers of the State Government are to be exercised in such a way as to ensure compliance with the laws made by Parliament. The Union Executive is also empowered to give such directions to a State as may appear necessary to the Government of India. Article 257 similarly provides that the executive power of every State shall be so exercised as not to impede the exercise of the executive power of the Union and the Union may issue necessary directions in that regard and for protection of railways and maintenance of means of communication of national or military importance. Any extra expenditure by the State for the purpose of fulfilling directives is to be reimbursed by the Union to the State. The provision in article 261, directing that full faith and credit shall be given to public acts, records and judicial proceedings of the Union and the States in all parts of the Indian territory, adds a lot to the smooth working of Union-State relations. Parliamentary control over inter-State rivers and provisions for adjudication of any inter-State water disputes were designed to take away friction between the Union and the States and between the States themselves (article 262).

The Constitution-makers did not want anything left to chance; hence the arrangements for inter-State Councils. Article 263 empowers the President to establish an Inter-State Council to enquire into and advise upon inter-State disputes and matters of common interest between States or between the Union and the States and make recommendations for better coordination of policy and action. Under article 258, the President may, with the consent of a State Government, entrust to that Government or its officers functions in relation to any matter to which the executive power of the Union extends. Under article 258A, the Governor of a State may, with the consent of the Union Government, entrust to that Government or to its officers functions in relation to any matter to which the executive power of the State extends.

Financial Relations

In regard to the financial relations between the Union and the States too, the Union may be said to be financially more powerful, but given the nature of the country's needs for growth through planned economy, this may be not only very desirable but entirely necessary. The States, however, have their own resources: the Union provides substantial amounts to the States by way of grants-in-aid, sharing proceeds of certain taxes, etc. The provision for the appointment of a Finance Commission every five years to examine the distribution of tax proceeds between the Union and the States and to determine the principles which should govern the grants-in-aid is an innovation of the Indian Constitution and has contributed to the generally smooth financial relationship between the Union and the States.

13

Emergency Provisions

Situations could arise under which it might not be possible for the normal scheme of the Constitution to function and it might then become necessary to suspend the operation of certain parts or provisions to protect the independence and the security of the nation and to safe-guard the Constitution and the democratic system. The Constitution envisages two kinds of emergencies, namely:

(i) a national emergency under article 352 due to threat of war, external aggression or armed rebellion, and

(ii) financial emergency under article 360.

The third kind of situation, that is the one under article 356 arising from a failure of the constitutional machinery in any particular state and necessitating President's Rule, though included under the Part on 'Emergency Provisions', may not strictly speaking be considered an emergency situation.

Every Proclamation of. Emergency is required to be laid before each House of Parliament, and is to cease to operate at the expiration of one month from the date of its issue by the President unless in the meantime it has been approved by resolutions of both the Houses. However, once approved by Parliament, the Proclamation may continue in operation for six months at a time unless revoked by the President earlier by a subsequent Proclamation. Resolutions approving the Proclamation of Emergency or its continuance have to be passed by either House of Parliament by a majority of the total membership and not less than two-thirds of those present and voting. Also, if the Lok Sabha passes a resolution disapproving the proclamation or its continuance, it shall be revoked forthwith. If notice of a resolution signed by not less than one-tenth of the total membership is given to the President Speaker, a special sitting of the House shall be held within 14 days to consider it.

Article 353 read with article 365 provides that once Emergency is proclaimed, the executive power of the Union extends to giving of directions to any State in regard to the exercise of the executive powers of the State and failure to comply with the directions would constitute enough justification for imposition of President's Rule under article 356.

During the operation of Emergency, the legislative power of Parliament also extends to conferring powers and imposing duties by law on union authorities in matters not otherwise included in the Union List.

There have been three proclamations of national emergency in India in October 1962 at the time of the Chinese aggression in India, in December 1971 in the wake of India's war with Pakistan, and in June 1975 on grounds of internal disturbance. During these periods of Emergency, extraordinary powers were assumed by the Union Government under several laws and constitutional amend merits passed by Parliament.

There was widespread criticism of the misuse of powers during the period of internal emergency. In the general elections that followed in 1997, the ruling Congress(I) under the leadership of Indira Gandhi lost and a Janata Party Government was formed—the first ever non-Congress government at the centre.

The provisions of article 352 were made more stringent in 1978- 79 by the Constitution (44th Amendment) Act, 1978 which came into effect from 20 June 1979. To prevent the misuse of emergency provisions, the words 'armed rebellion' were substituted for 'internal disturbance', a written communication of the decision by the Union Cabinet was made an essential pre-condition for the issue of a Proclamation by the President, and the entire procedure for emergency provisions was streamlined to ensure dependence on approval of Parliament, particularly of the Lok Sabha. Thus, the Amendment confined the suspension of article 19 only to situations of war or external aggression, i.e. where emergency was proclaimed on internal grounds of 'armed rebellion', freedoms under article 19 could not be taken away. Also, the same amendment laid down that under no circumstances could the enforcement of rights under articles 20 and 21 be denied even during an Emergency.

President's Rule

It is the constitutional duty of the Union to protect its States against external aggression and internal disturbance and to ensure that the Government of every State is carried on in accordance with the Constitution (article 355).

If on receipt of a Report from the Governor or otherwise, the President is satisfied that Government of the State cannot be carried on in accordance with the Constitution or that the constitutional machinery has failed, he may issue a proclamation taking over any of the functions and powers of the State Government including those of the Governor and other State authorities (article 356). The satisfaction of the President, of course, means the satisfaction of the Union Government and President's rule is actually rule by the Union Government.

It is important that article 356 is read with articles 355, 256, 257, 353 and 365. This is usually not done.

Insofar as article 355 speaks of the duty of the Union to ensure that government of every state is carried on in accordance with the provisions of the Constitution, it is obvious that article 356 is not the only one to take care of a situation of failure of constitutional machinery. The Union can also act under article 355 i.e. without imposing President's rule. Article 355 can stand on its own. Also, Union Government can issue certain directions under articles 256, 257 and 353.

Article 356 clearly authorises the President to issue a proclamation imposing President's Rule over a State if he is satisfied that a situation has arisen in which the Government of the State cannot be carried on in accordance with the provisions of this Constitution—but a question may be asked—when can the President lawfully hold that such a situation has actually arisen. A very specific and categorical answer is contained in article 365 when it says that where a State fails to comply with Union directions (under articles 256, 257 and others) 'it shall be lawful for the President to hold that a situation has arisen in which the Government of the State cannot be carried on in accordance with the provisions of this Constitution'. It is unfortunate that before rushing to issue proclamations under article 356, no effort appeared to have been made to ensure that (i) the Union had done all that it could in discharge of its duty under article 355 and (ii) that the State had 'failed to comply with, or give effect to' those directions. It seems in many cases recourse to 356 was taken without keeping other provisions in view.

Article 356, enabling the imposition of President's rule over the States by the Union, has been one of the most criticised and controversial provisions of the Constitution. Under this provision, State Governments have been taken over by the Union on nearly 115 occasions. Dr. Ambedkar had expressed the hope that it might remain a dead letter and might never be used except as a last resort, after everything else failed.

In the Bommai case, the Court went much further. It was held (i) that the question of the State Government losing the confidence of the House should be decided on the floor of the House and until that is done the Ministry should not be unseated, (ii) that dissolution of the Assembly by Presidential Proclamation is subject to judicial review, and (iii) that if the court finds that relevant material justifying the proclamation did not exist or that malafide was involved, it may strike it down and restore the Ministry [Bommai vs Union of India, JT (1994) 2 SC 215].

Financial Emergency

The President is authorised by article 360 of the Constitution to declare by a proclamation Financial Emergency if he is satisfied that the financial stability or credit of India or of any part of its territory is threatened. Such a proclamation may be revoked or varied by a subsequent proclamation. It has to be laid before both Houses of Parliament and ceases to operate at the expiration of two months unless meanwhile approved by resolutions of the two Houses. Once approved by Parliament, unlike proclamations under article 352, it may continue indefinitely until revoked or varied.

Thus far, during the operation of the Constitution, there has been no occasion for the promulgation of Financial Emergency.

14

Elections

Part XV, articles 324 to 329A of the Constitution provide for elections. Representative parliamentary democracy calls for a system of choosing representatives of the people and for a suitable machinery for the purpose. The Constitution provides for universal Adult Franchise. Every citizen of India who is 18 years or above has full voting rights, irrespective of religion, race, caste, sex, or place of birth. It is most important that the elections are free and fair and are seen to be so. In a country of India's vast size, its large population and with a massive electorate, the conduct of nation-wide elections becomes a gigantic undertaking [articles 324(1), 325 and 326].

It has been said that holding general elections in India is equal to holding them for Europe, United States, Canada and Australia all put together.

Constitution empowers the Parliament to make laws concerning elections to either House of Parliament or to either House of the Legislature of a State, including the preparation of electoral rolls, the delimitation of constituencies and all other necessary matters for securing the due constitution of such House or Houses (article 327). The Representation of the People Act, 1950 and the Representation of the People Act, 1951 are two of the most important statutes enacted in pursuance of this provision. Supplementing the provisions of these statutes are the Registration of Electoral Rules, 1960 and the Conduct of Election Rules, 1961. The Acts and Rules are amended and updated from time to time to meet the exigencies of developing situations. Article 328 confers powers on State Legislaturesto make laws relating to elections to the House, or either House of the State Legislature.

Article 329 seeks to bar interference by courts in electoral matters, including:

(i) the validity of any law relating to delimitation of constituencies or the allotment of seats under article 327 or 328, and
(ii) election to either House of Parliament or a State Legislature.

The latter can be questioned only by an election petition presented to such authority and in such manner as may be provided by law by the concerned legislature. Under the Representation of the People Act, the power to decide election disputes now vests in the High Courts with a right of appeal to the Supreme Court. Disputes relating to the election of the President or Vice-President are, however, to be settled by the Supreme Court.

Election Commission

The Constitution provides for an Election Commission to superintend, direct and control all elections to Parliament, the State Legislatures, and to the offices of the President and the Vice-President. The Election Commission shall consist of the Chief Election Commissioner and such number of other Election commissioners, if any, as the President may from time to time fix.

Article 324 also provides for the appointment of Regional Commissioners at the time of General Elections after consultation with the Chief Election Commissioner. The Chief Election Commissioner cannot be removed from his office except in like manner and on like grounds as a Judge of the Supreme Court and the conditions of his service cannot be varied to his disadvantage after his appointment. Other Election Commissioners, if any, can be removed only on the recommendation of the Chief Election Commissioner.

Electoral Reforms: The 17 general elections to Lok Sabha and a much plarger number for different State Assemblies etc have been universally held to be free and fair. Several electoral reforms have been talked about in academia, media, National Commissions and Committees from time to time. At least one reform suggestion that has been under the active consideration of the Government for some time is that of simultaneous elections for Lok Sabha and all State Assemblies.

15

Local Self-Government Institutions

Panchayati Raj

Giving expression to Gandhiji's basic views on the structure of India's polity, the President of the Constituent Assembly, Dr. Rajendra Prasad had expressed himself strongly in favour of the idea of 'making the Constitution begin with the village and go up' from there with adult franchise being utilised only for the village panchayats which could, in turn, act as the electoral college for electing representatives at the State and Union levels.

A new orientation and constitutional status was accorded to the local self government institution at the level of towns and villages by the 73rd and 74th constitutional amendments.

Articles 40 under the Directive Principles had provided a compromise or a concession to Gandhi's views. It was included under the non-enforceable Part V on the Directive Principles of State Policy. It is said that State shall take steps to organize village panchayats and endow them with necessary authority 'to function as units of self-government'.

The 73rd and 74th constitutional amendments made some fundamental changes in Indian political structure and in the status of local institutions. The two amendments provide for the state legislatures making their own laws under the constitutional provisions for establishing panchayats, municipalities, etc. and conferring on them such powers and authority as may be necessary to enable them to function as institutions of self-government. In every state, a three-tier system is envisaged. Panchayats are to be established at the village and district levels and at the intermediate level. States which have a population of less than two million, need not have the intermediate level of panchayats.

The important thing was that panchayats had to be elected directly by the people in the same manner as members of the popular houses at the Union and State levels are elected, i.e. through territorial constituencies. For a village panchayat, the electorate would be the Gram Sabha which would consist of those registered in the electoral rolls. These panchayats cannot remain superceded for long; fresh elections would have to be held within six months of the dissolution of a panchayat. Secondly, in all panchayats, seats would be reserved for women, Scheduled Castes and Scheduled Tribes. There shall be a fixed five year term for all panchayats. They shall have their own budget, power of taxation and list of items in their jurisdiction. In their respective areas, the panchayats shall be able to formulate their own development plans and implement them. Every State shall have a State Election Commissioner for conducting panchayat elections and every five years a State Finance Commission shall he constituted to take stock of the economic conditions of the Panchayats.

Similarly, in the 74th amendment, there are provisions for the set-ting up of nagarpalikas and nagar panchayats. In the matter of reservations, election, power of taxation, formulation and implementation of development projects, constitution of a Finance Commission, fixed term, etc., the provision are very similar to those in the 73rd amendment in respect of panchayats.

The salient features of the 73rd Amendment Act, 1992 were:

- To provide 3-tier system of Panchayati Raj for all states having population of over 20 lakh.
- To hold panchayat elections regularly every 5 years.
- To provide reservation of seats for Scheduled Castes, Scheduled Tribes and women.
- To appoint state finance commission to make recommendations as regards the financial powers of the panchayats.
- To constitute District Planning Committee to prepare draft development plan for the district as a whole.

The following powers and responsibilities were to be delegated to panchayats at the appropriate level:

- Preparation of plan for economic development and social justice.
- Implementation of schemes for economic development and social justice in relation to 29 subjects given in the Eleventh Schedule of the Constitution.
- To levy, collect and appropriate taxes, duties, tolls and fees.

The 74th Constitution Amendment Act, 1992 came into force on 1 June 1993. All the State governments passed the conformity legislation and brought it into force within the constitutionally stipulated deadline of 1 June, 1994. The amending laws of the existing municipal legislations have provided for regularity of elections, representation and reservations. The new laws under the Constitution have made municipal elections mandatory every five years. Some of the important features of the Act are as follows:

1. Devolution of more functions and taxation powers.
2. Revenue sharing with State government funds.

3. Regular conduct of elections.
4. Reservation of seats for Scheduled Castes, Scheduled Tribes and for women.
5. Uniform composition of the urban bodies throughout the country.
6. Prescription of criteria for categorising urban local bodies like town panchayat, municipalities, city municipal corporations.
7. Restriction on the formation of townships only to industrial areas where the entire municipal services are provided or proposed to be provided by the industry.
8. Formation of District Planning and Metropolitan Planning Committee.

16

Unique Features of India's Constitution

Our Constitution is unique in many ways. It does not actually fit into any of the existing models.

The Lengthiest

Talking of the many unique features, the thing usually mentioned first is that of its sheer physical size; it is the world's lengthiest Constitution ever given to a nation.

Written and Unwritten

Constitution of a country may be written or unwritten. We have a written Constitution but unwritten conventions developed and carried forward from the colonial period or evolved since the commencement of the Constitution also remain relevant and guide the actual working of the Constitution.

Rigid and Flexible

Constitutions are classified as rigid or flexible on the basis of easy or difficult amending process. India's Constitution adopts a mixed procedure where under some changes can be brought about by the Union Parliament by simple majority vote while certain category of amendments require a special majority support in the two houses of Parliament. Then, there are certain provisions which cannot be amended without the consent of States. The Supreme Court has added yet another category by its doctrine of basic features under which any amendment altering the basic structure or features of the Constitution shall be void. Thus, our Constitution is both rigid and flexible.

Federal and Unitary

Depending on the structure of the polity, relations between the central authority and units, distribution of powers etc, Constitutions may be divided as federal or unitary. India's Constitution has been variously described as quasi-federal, federal with a strong unitary or pro-centre bias, federal in structure but unitary in spirit, federal in normal times but with possibilities of being converted into a purely unitary one during Emergency, etc. The fact is, it has features of both. It cannot be considered unitary because it provides, for example, for distribution of executive and legislative powers between the Union and the States, and provisions affecting the powers of the States or Union-State relations cannot be amended without ratification by the States. It cannot be considered strictly federal either because the residuary powers vest in the Union. As Dr. Ambedkar said, rigidity and legalism were the two serious weaknesses of federalism.

Under Article 249, the Union Parliament can invade the State List. Under Articles 356 and 357, on the ground of failure of constitutional machinery in any State, all its executive and legislative powers may be taken over by the Union; and under

Articles 352 to 354, the Constitution can be converted into an entirely unitary one inasmuch as during Proclamation of Emergency, the executive and legislative powers of the Union extend to matters even in the State List. Finally, under Articles 2, 3 and 4, new States may be formed, and areas, boundaries or names of existing States altered by the Union Parliament by ordinary law passed by simple majority votes. One may say that the polity of India is both federal and unitary or a mix of the two. Dr. Ambedkar said in the Constituent Assembly:

> "Though the country and the people may be divided into different States for convenience of administration, the country is one integral whole, it's people a single people living under a single imperium derived from a single source".

Presidential and Parliamentary

India is a Republic and the head is the President in whom all the executive power vests and in whose name it is to be exercised. He is also the Supreme Commander of the armed forces. On the other hand, we have accepted the system of parliamentary democracy with ministerial responsibility to the popular House of Parliament. Again, we have features of both Presidential and Parliamentary.

Parliamentary Sovereignty and Judicial Supremacy

In India, the Constitution has arrived at a middle course and a compromise between the British sovereignty of Parliament and American judicial supremay. Since we have a written constitution and the powers and functions of every organ are defined and delimited by the Constitution, there is no question of any organ—not even Parliament, being sovereign. Both Parliament and the Supreme Court are supreme in their respective spheres. While the Supreme Court may declare a law passed by Parliament ultra vires as being violative of the Constitution, Parliament may, within certain restrictions, amend most parts of the Constitution.

Longest Lasting

Of all the Constitutions of nations adopted after the Second World War, India's Constitution has proved to be the longest lasting. It has also emerged as the single strongest force for national unity and integrity.

Annexure

Table of Constitutional Amendments (1950-2021)

Constitution Amendment Act No., Year	Provisions Amendment/ inserted/ Replaced	Main effect of amendment
1. The Constitution (First Amendment) Act, 1951	15, 19, 31A, 31B, 85, 87, 174, 176, 341, 342, 372, 376 & 9th Schedule	More restrictions on freedoms under article 19 on grounds of maintenance of public order, friendly relations with foreign states, protecting land reform legislation and State's right to carry on any trade, business, industry, service etc. to the exclusion of others.
2. The Constitution (Second Amendment) Act, 1952	81	Reducing representation in Lok Sabha by omitting the provision of "not less than one member for every 7,50,000 of the population."
3. The Constitution (Third Amendment) Act, 1954	7th Schedule	Powers to the Union to control the production, supply and distribution of some essential commodities.
4. The Constitution (Fourth Amendment) Act, 1955	31, 31A, 305 & 9th Schedule	State's powers of compulsory acquisition of private property and of providing for State monopoly in certain trades etc reasserted. Adequacy of compensation not to be questioned. More Acts placed beyond judicial review by

		being included in the 9th Schedule.
5. The Constitution (Fifth Amendment) Act, 1955.	3	Requiring the State Legislatures concerned to give their views under article 3 within a specified period.
6. The Constitution (Sixth Amendment) Act, 1956	269, 286 and 7th Schedule	Inter-State sales and purchase tax on trade and commerce (except for newspapers) moved to the Union level.
7. The Constitution (Seventh Amendment) Act, 1956	1, 81, 82, 131, 153, 158, 168, 170, 171, 216, 217, 220, 222, 224, 230, 231, 232, 258A, 290A, 298, 350A, 350B, 371, 372A, 378A, and 1st, 2nd, 4th and 8th Schedules	Implementing the States' reorganisation scheme, ending the Parts A, B and C categories having only 14 States and 6 Union Territories.
8. The Constitution (Eighth Amendment) Act, 1960	334	Extending the reservations in Lok Sabha and State Assemblies for SC and ST and for Anglo-Indians for another 10 years.
9. The Constitution (Ninth Amendment) Act, 1960	1st Schedule	Enabling transfer of certain territories under the Indo-Pak agreement.
10. The Constitution (Tenth Amendment) Act, 1961	240 and 1st Schedule	Including areas of Dadra and Nagar Haveli as a Union Territory.
11. The Constitution (Eleventh Amendment) Act, 1961	66, 71	Providing that the election of President or Vice President could not be challenged on the ground of any vacancy in the appropriate electoral college.
12. The Constitution (Twelfth Amendment) Act, 1962	240 and 1st Schedule	Including Goa, Daman and Diu as a Union Territory.
13. The Constitution (Thirteenth Amendment) Act, 1962	Part XXI	Making special provisions for the State of Nagaland.

14. The Constitution (Fourteenth Amendment) Act, 1962	81, 240, 239A and 1st and 4th Schedule	Including Pondicherry as a Union Territory.
15. The Constitution (Fifteenth Amendmesnt) Act, 1963	124, 128, 217, 222, 224, 226, 297, 311, 316, 224A and 7th Schedule	Increasing the age of retirement of High Court judges and provision of compensatory allowance to judges transferred from one High Court to another, appointment of retired judges to act as judges of High Court and extending the writ jurisdiction of High Courts.
16. The Constitution (Sixteenth Amendment) Act, 1963	19, 84, 173 and 3rd Schedule	Further restriction on the rights to freedom of speech and expression, to assemble peaceably and without arms and to form associations in the interests of sovereignty and integrity of India, oath or affirmation to be subscribed by candidates seeking election to Parliament and State Legislatures amended to include as one of the conditions that day will uphold the sovereignty and integrity of India.
17. The Constitution (Seventeenth Amendment) Act, 1964	31A and 9th Schedule	Prohibiting the acquisition of land under personal cultivation unless the market value of the land is paid as compensation. Putting 44 more Acts under the 9th Schedule.
18. The Constitution (Eighteenth Amendment) Act, 1966	3	'State' in article 3 to include Union territory, power to form a new State or Union territory to include the power to do so by uniting a part of a State or Union territory to another.

19. The Constitution (Nineteenth Amendment) Act, 1966	324	Abolition of Election Tribunals, High Courts to hear election petitions.
20. The Constitution (Twentieth Amendment) Act, 1966	233A	Validating some appointments of district judges.
21. The Constitution (Twenty-first Amendment) Act, 1967	8th Schedule	Inclusion of 'Sindhi' language in the 8th Schedule.
22. The Constitution (Twenty-second Amendment) Act, 1969	244A, 275 and 371B	Formation of a new autonomous state of Meghalaya within state of Assam.
23. The Constitution (Twenty-third Amendment) Act, 1969	330, 332, 333, 334	Reservation of seats in Parliament and State Legislatures for Scheduled Castes and Scheduled Tribes as well as for Anglo-Indians for a further period of ten years.
24. The Constitution (Twenty-fourth Amendment) Act, 1971	13, 368	To remove all doubts regarding the power of Parliament to amend the Constitution including the Fundamental Rights.
25. The Constitution (Twenty-fifth Amendment) Act, 1971	31, 31C	Substituting the word 'amount' in place of 'compensation' in the light of the judicial interpretation of the word 'compensation' meaning 'adequate compensation'.
26. The Constitution (Twenty-sixth Amendment) Act, 1971	291, 362, 363A, 366	Abolition of the privy purses and privileges of former rulers of princely States.
27. The Constitution (Twenty-seventh Amendment) Act, 1971	239A, 239B, 240, 371C	To provide for certain matters necessitated by the reorganisation of north-eastern states and enabling the promulgation of Ordinances by Administrators of certain Union Territories.

28. The Constitution (Twenty-eighth Amendment) Act, 1972	312A, 314	To abolish the special privileges of the members of Indian Civil Services in matters of leave, pension and rights in regard to disciplinary matters.
29. The Constitution (Twenty-ninth Amendment) Act, 1972	9th Schedule	Including two more (Kerala) Acts in the 9th Schedule.
30. The Constitution (Thirtieth Amendment) Act, 1972	133	To do away with the valuation test of Rs. 20,000 and to provide for an appeal to Supreme Court only on a certificate issued by High Court that the case involves a substantial question of law of general importance and that in the opinion of the High Court, the question needs to be decided by the Supreme Court.
31. The Constitution (Thirty-first Amendment) Act, 1973	81, 330, 332	Raising the upper limit for the representation of States in the Lok Sabha from 500 to 525 and reducing the upper limit for the representation of Union territories from 25 members to 20.
32. The Constitution (Thirty-second Amendment) Act, 1973	371, 371D, 371E and 7th Schedule	Giving effect to the provision of equal opportunities to different areas of the State of Andhra Pradesh, the Constitution of an Administrative Tribunal with jurisdiction to deal with grievances relating to public services and empowering Parliament to legislate for the establishment of a Central University in the State.
33. The Constitution (Thirty-third Amendment) Act, 1974	101, 190 and 9th Schedule	To streamline the procedure for resignation of Members of Parliament and State Legislatures.

34. The Constitution (Thirty-fourth Amendment) Act, 1974	9th Schedule	Twenty more land tenure and land reform laws enacted by various State Legislatures included in the Ninth Schedule.
35. The Constitution (Thirty-fifth Amendment) Act, 1974	2A, 80, 81 and 10th Schedule	Conferring on Sikkim the status of an associate State of Indian Union.
36. The Constitution (Thirty-sixth Amendment) Act, 1975	2A, 80, 81, 371F and 1st, 461 and 10th Schedule	To make Sikkim a full-fledged State of Indian Union and to allot to Sikkim one seat each in the Council of States and in the House of the People.
37. The Constitution (Thirty-seventh Amendment) Act, 1975	239A, 240	Provision of a Legislative Assembly for the Union Territory of Aruna-chal Pradesh.
38. The Constitution (Thirty-eighth Amendment) Act, 1975	123, 213, 239B, 352, 356, 359, 360	To provide that the satisfaction of President or Governor would not be called in question in any court of law.
39. The Constitution (Thirty-ninth Amendment) Act, 1975	71, 329, 329A and 9th Schedule	Disputes relating to the election of the President, Vice President, Prime Minister and Speaker to be determined by such authority as may be determined by Parliamentary Law. Certain Central enactments also included in the 9th Schedule.
40. The Constitution (Fortieth Amendment) Act, 1976	297 and 9th Schedule	Vesting in the Union of all mines, mineralc and other things of value lying in the ocean within the territorial waters or the continental shelf or the exclusive economic zone of India. Limits of the territorial waters, the continental shelf, the exclusive economic zone and the maritime zones of India to be as specified from time to time. Some more Acts were added to the 9th Schedule.

41. The Constitution (Forty-first Amendmenst) Act, 1976	316	To raise the retirement age of Members of State Public Service Commissions and Joint Public Service Commissions from 60 to 62 years.
42. The Constitution (Forty-second Amendment) Act, 1976	31, 31C, 31D, 32A, 39, 39A, 43A, 48A, 55, 74, 77, 81, 82, 83, 100, 102, 103, 105, 118, 145, 150, 166, 170, 172, 189, 191, 192, 194, 208, 217, 225, 226, 226A, 227, 228, 228A, 257A, 311, 312, 330, 352, 353, 356, 357, 358, 359, 366, 368, 371F, and Parts IVA & XIVA	Specifically including in the Preamble the ideal of socialism, secularism and integrity of the nation, to make the Directive Principles more comprehensive and giving them precedence over Fundamental Rights. Inserting a new chapter on the Fundamental Duties of citizens and special provisions for dealing with anti-national activities, whether by individuals or by associations. Providing for a minimum number of judges for determining questions as to the constitutional validity of laws and for a special majority of not less than two-third for declaring any law to be constitutionally invalid. To reduce the mounting arrears in High Courts and to secure the speedy disposal of service matters, revenue matters and certain other matters of special importance in the context of socio-economic development and progress, creation of Administrative and other tribunals for dealing with such matters.
43. The Constitution (Forty-third Amendment) Act, 1977	31D, 32A, 131A, 144A, 145, 226, 226A, 228, 228A, 366	Restoration of the jurisdiction of the Supreme Court and High Courts, curtailed by the enactment of the Constitution

		(Forty-second Amendment) Act, 1976; omission of article 31D regarding saving of laws in respect of anti-national activities.
44. The Constitution (Forty-fourth Amendment) Act, 1978	19, 22, 30, 31, 31A, 31C, 38, 71, 74, 77, 83, 103, 105, 123, 132, 133, 134, 134A, 139A, 150, 166, 172, 192, 194, 213, 217, 225, 226, 227, 239B, 257A, 329, 329A, 352, 356, 358, 359, 360, 361A, 371F, 9th Schedule and Chapter IV in Part XII	Right to property omitted as a fundamental right; "armed rebellion" and not merely "internal disturbance" made a necessary ground for proclamation of emergency, preventive detention not to be authorised beyond two months without the decision of the Advisory Board, removing various distortions brought about by the 42nd Amendment.
45. The Constitution (Forty-fifth Amendment) Act, 1980	334	To extend reservation of seats in Parliament and State Assemblies for Scheduled Castes, Scheduled Tribes as well as for Anglo-Indians for a further period of ten years.
46. The Constitution (Forty-sixth Amendment) Act, 1982	269, 286, 366 and 7th Schedule	To enable Parliament to formulate by law principle for determining when a consignment of goods takes place in the course of inter-state trade or commerce. To enable the levy of tax on the consignment of goods where such consignment takes place in the course of inter-state trade or commerce. To enable Parliament to specify, by law, restrictions and conditions in regard to the system of levy rates and other incidence of tax on the transfer of goods involved in the execution of a works contract, on the

		delivery of goods on hire-purchase or any system of payment in instalments. To insert a definition of "tax on the sale or purchase of goods" to include transfer for consideration of controlled commodities, transfer of property in goods involved in the execution of a works contract, delivery of goods on hire-purchase or any system of payment by instalments, etc.
47. The Constitution (Forty-seventh Amendment) Act, 1984	9th Schedule	To provide for the inclusion of certain land Reform Acts in the Ninth Schedule.
48. The Constitution (Forty-eighth Amendment) Act, 1984	356	To provide for continuation of President's rule in Punjab beyond the prescribed limit of one year.
49. The Constitution (Forty-ninth Amendment) Act, 1984	244 and 5th and 6th Schedule	To give a constitutional security to the autonomous District Council functioning in the State of Tripura.
50. The Constitution (Fiftieth Amendment) Act, 1984	33	Restrictions on fundamental rights extended to members of the force charged with protection of State property, to members of intelligence and counter-intelligence groups of the State, and to those in the telecommunication systems.
51. The Constitution (Fifty-first Amendment) Act, 1984	330, 332	Providing reservation of seats for Scheduled Tribes in Meghalaya, Nagaland, Arunachal Pradesh and Mizoram in Parliament and to provide similar reservation in the Legislative Assemblies of Nagaland and Meghalaya to meet the aspirations of local tribal population.

52. The Constitution (Fifty-second Amendment) Act, 1985	101, 102, 190, 191 and 10th Schedule	To provide that a Member of Parliament or a State Legislature who defects from the party which set him up as a candidate in the election or if an independent member of the House joins a political party shall be disqualified to remain a member of the House unless covered under provision of party splits or mergers.
53. The Constitution (Fifty-third Amendment) Act, 1986	71G	Preventing application of any Act of Parliament in Mizorarn in respect of religious or social practices of Mizos, Mizos' customary law and procedure, administration of civil and criminal practice involving decisions according to Mizos' customary law and ownership and transfer of land unless a resolution is passed in the Legislative Assembly to that effect.
54. The Constitution (Fifty-fourth Amendment) Act, 1986	125, 221 and 2nd Schedule	Increasing the salaries of Chief Justice and Judges of the Supreme Court to Rs.10,000 and Rs. 9,000 p.m. respectively and of the C.J. and Judges of High Courts to Rs. 9,000 and Rs. 8,000 p.m. respectively.
55. The Constitution (Fifty-fifth Amendment) Act, 1986	371H	To confer statehood on the Union Territory of Arunachal Pradesh and to vest special responsibility on Governor with respect to law and order in the State. The Legislative Assembly of the new State of Arunachal Pradesh to consist of not less than thirty members.

56. The Constitution (Fifty-sixth Amendment) Act, 1987	371I	To constitute the territories comprised in Goa District of the Union Territory of Goa, Daman and Diu and to provide that the Legislative Assembly of the new State of Goa shall consist of not less than 30 members.
57. The Constitution (Fifty-seventh Amendment) Act, 1987	332 (3A)	To provide for reservation of seats in the House of the People for Scheduled Tribes in Nagaland, Meghalaya, Mizoram and Arunachal Pradesh for a temporary period until the re-adjustment of seats on the basis of first census after the year 2000.
58. The Constitution (Fifty-eighth Amendment) Act, 1987	394A and heading of Part XXII	Authorising the publication of an authentic Hindi text of the Constitution and of constitutional amendments.
59. The Constitution (Fifty-ninth Amendment) Act, 1988	356, 359A	Continuation of President's rule in Punjab up to 3 years.
60. The Constitution (Sixtieth Amendment) Act, 1988	276	To increase the ceiling of taxes on professions, trades, callings and employment from Rs. 250 per annum to Rs. 2500 per annum.
61. The Constitution (Sixty-first Amendment) Act, 1989	326	Reducing voting age from 21 to 18 years.
62. The Constitution (Sixty-second Amendment) Act, 1989	334	To continue the reservation for the Scheduled Castes and the Scheduled Tribes and the representation of the Anglo-Indians by nomination for a further period of 10 years.
63. The Constitution (Sixty-third Amendment) Act, 1989	356, 359A	Omitting the special provision re- proclamation of emergency and for continuation of President's rule in Punjab.

64. The Constitution (Sixty-fourth Amendment) Act, 1990	356	To facilitate the extension of the proclamation up to a total period of three years and six months in relation to the State of Punjab.
65. The Constitution (Sixty-fifth Amendment) Act, 1990	338	In place of the existing special officer for ST & SC, constitution of a National Commission for Scheduled Castes and Scheduled Tribes consisting of a Chairperson, Vice-Chairperson and five other Members.
66. The Constitution (Sixty-sixth Amendment) Act, 1990	9th Schedule	Including another set of 55 State Acts in the 9th Schedule.
67. The Constitution (Sixty-seventh Amendment) Act, 1990	356	To further extend the period of proclamation in respect of Punjab to four years.
68. The Constitution (Sixty-eighth Amendment) Act, 1991	356	To further extend the period of proclamation in respect of Punjab to 5 years.
69. The Constitution (Sixty-ninth Amendment) Act, 1991	239AA, 239AB	Legislative Assembly and a Council of Ministers and give a special status to this Union Territory as the National Capital Territory.
70. The Constitution (Seventieth Amendment) Act, 1992	54, 239AA	To provide that reference to 'State' in Article 54 and 55 would include the National Capital Territory of Delhi and the Union Territory of Pondicherry for constituting the electoral college for election of the President, to enable the elected members of the Legislative Assemblies of Pondicherry and Delhi to be included in the electoral college.

71. The Constitution (Seventy-first Amendment) Act, 1992	8th Schedule	To include Konkani, Manipuri and Nepali languages in the Eighth Schedule.
72. The Constitution (Seventy-second Amendment) Act, 1992	332	For making a temporary provision for the determination of the number of seats reserved for the Scheduled Tribes in the State Assembly of Tripura, until the re-adjustment of seats is made on the basis of the first Census after the year 2000.
73. The Constitution (Seventy-third Amendment) Act, 1992	280, 11th Schedule and Part IX	To insert a whole new Part IX relating to village Panchayats, direct elections to all seats in Panchayats at the village and intermediate level, if any and to the offices of Chairpersons of Panchayats at such levels; reservation of seats for the Scheduled Castes and Scheduled Tribes in proportion to their population for membership of Panchayats and office of Chairpersons in Panchayats at each level; reservation of not less than one-third of the seats for women; fixing tenure of five years for Panchayats and holding elections within a period of six months in the event of supersession of any Panchayat.
74. The Constitution (Seventy-fouth Amendment) Act, 1992	280, 12th Schedule and Part IXA	Adding a new Part IXA relating to the Municipalities to provide for among other things, constitution of three types of Municipalities, i.e., Nagar Panchayats for areas in transition from a rural area to

		urban area. Municipal Councils for smaller urban areas and Municipal Corporations for larger urban areas.
75. The Constitution (Seventy-fifth Amendment) Act, 1993	323B	To give timely relief to the rent litigants by providing for setting up of state-level Rent Tribunals in order to reduce the tiers of appeals and to exclude the jurisdiction of all courts, except that of the Supreme Court.
76. The Constitution (Seventy-sixth Amendment) Act, 1994	9th Schedule	To protect Tamil Nadu law extending reservation to 69% [18% for SC, 1% ST and 50% OBCs] by including it in the 9th Schedule.
77. The Constitution (Seventy-seventh Amendment) Act, 1995	16	To continue the existing policy of reservation in promotion for the Scheduled Castes and the Scheduled Tribes by inserting a new clause (4A) in article 16 to provide for reservation in promotion for the Scheduled Castes and the Scheduled Tribes.
78. The Constitution (Seventh-eighth Amendment) Act, 1995	9th Schedule	To include a number of amending Acts along with a few principal Acts in the 9th Schedule so as to ensure that implementation of these Acts is not adversely affected by litigation.
79. The Constitution (Seventy-ninth Amendment) Act, 1999	334	To extend the reservations of seats for the Scheduled Castes and the Scheduled Tribes as well as for the Anglo-Indians in the House of the People and in the Legislative Assemblies of the States for another 10 years.

80. The Constitution (Eightieth Amendment) Act, 2000	269, 270, 272	To give effect to the new scheme for sharing revenues recommended by the 10th Finance Commission. Under the new scheme of devolution of revenue between the Union and the States, 26 per cent out of gross proceeds of Union taxes and duties is to be assigned to the States in lieu of eetheir existing share in the income-tax, excise duties, special excise duties and grants in lieu of tax on railway passenger fares.
81. The Constitution (Eighty-first Amendment) Act, 2000	16	To regard unfilled seats reserved for SC & ST as a separate class of vacancies under article 16 to be filled up in any succeeding year or years and not to be considered together with the vacancies of the year in which they were filled up for determining the ceiling of fifty per cent reservation against total number of vacancies of that year.
82. The Constitution (Eighty-second Amendment) Act, 2000	335	Making provision in favour of the members of the Scheduled Castes and the Scheduled Tribes for relaxation in qualifying marks in any examination or lowering the standards evaluation for reservation. In matters of promotion to any class or classes of services or posts in connection with affairs of the Union or of a State.
83. The Constitution (Eighty-third Amendment) Act, 2000	243M	To provide that no reservation in Panchayats need be made in favour of the Scheduled

		Castes in Arunachal Pradesh wholly inhabited by tribal population.
84. The Constitution (Eighty-fourth Amendment) Act, 2001	55, 81 170, 330, 332	To provide (a) that reference fourth Amendment) Act, to 'population of the State' in 2001 articles concerning elections to the office of the President and to Lok Sabha shall continue to mean population as ascertained by the 1971 census until the census after 2026, (b) that until 2026 the allocation of seats in Lok Sabha to the States shall continue to be on the basis of 1971 census but the constituencies within each State may be readjusted on the basis of 1991 census, and (c) that reservation of seats in the Lok Sabha and State Assemblies for SC/ST shall be on the basis of the 1991 census until after 2026.
85. The Constitution (Eighty-fifth Amendment) Act, 2001	16	To allow provision for reservation in matters of promotion with consequential seniority in services under the State for SC/ST employees.
86. The Constitution (Eighty-sixth Amendment) Act, 2002	21A, 45, 51A	To insert a new article 21A to provide for a fundamental right to education to all children of 6 to 14 years. Also, it substitutes article 45 in the Directive Principles by a new article providing for early child care and education to children below 6 years. By amending article 51A, a new fundamental duty is sought to be

		added for parents or guardians providing educational opportunities to children below the age of 6 and 14 years.
87. The Constitution (Eighty-seventh Amendment) Act, 2003 21A, 45, 51A	81, 82, 170, 330	To substitute the figure 2001 for the figure 1991 in the provisos to articles 81, 82, 170 and 330 thereby laying down that the population figures to be taken into account for purposes of readjusting constituencies within each State and for reservation of seats in the Lok Sabha and State Assemblies for SC/ST shall be on the basis of 2001 census.
88. The Constitution (Eighty-eighth Amendment) Act, 2003	268A, 7th Schedule	To add new article 268A to provide for levy of taxes on services to be collected and appropriated by the Government of India and the States, to insert new entry "92C. Taxes on Services" to the Union List, 7th Schedule.
89. The Constitution (Eighty-ninth Amendment) Act, 2003	338, 338A	To amend article 338 and add a new article 338A to provide for two separate Commissions for Scheduled Castes and Scheduled Tribes.
90. The Constitution (Ninetieth Act, 2003 Constitution Amendment)	332	To amend article 332 to provide for maintaining the erstwhile representation of the Scheduled Tribes and Non-Scheduled Tribes in Assam constituencies included in Bodoland Territorial Area District.
91. The Constitution (Ninety-first Amendment) Act, 2003	75, 164, 361B and 10th Schedule	To amend articles 75, 164 and Schedule 10, to insert a new article 361B, to place a limit on the number of Ministers

		not to be more than 15% of the House of the People at the Union level and Vidhan Sabha at the level of States; to take away the protection from defectors on grounds of splits and make defectors disqualified from Membership and ineligible for Ministership or other remunerative political post till re-elections.
92. The Constitution (Ninety-second Amendment) Act, 2003	8th Schedule	To add four more languages viz. Bodo, Dogri, Santhali and Maithili to the existing 18.
93. The Constitution (Ninety-third Amendment) Act, 2005	15	To make a special provision by law for socially and educationally backward classes, SC & STs in regard to admission to educational institutions including private—aided or unaided—institutions other than minority institutions.
94. The Constitution (Ninety-fourth Amendment) Act, 2006	164	To amend proviso to article 164(1) to substitute the words "Chhattisgarh, Jharkhan.d" in place of the word "Bihar" as there were now no scheduled areas in Bihar left after the creation of Jharkhand.
95. The Constitution (Ninety-fifth Amendment) Act, 2009	334	To extend the provision for reservation of seats of SC/ST and Anglo-Indians in House of the People and State Assemblies for another 10 years.
96. The Constitution (Ninety-sixth Amendment) Act, 2011	8th Schedule	To Substitute 'Oriya' in the 8th Schedule by 'Odia'.

97. The Constitution (Ninety-seventh Amendment) Act, 2011	19, 43B, 243ZH to 243ZT, PART IXB	To provide for promotion and functioning of Cooperative societies.
98. The Constitution (Ninety-eighth Amendment) Act, 2012	371J	To insert new article 371J to make special provision for empowering the Governor in regard to Hydera-bad-Karnataka region.
99. The Constitution (Ninety-ninth Amendment) Act, 2014	124, 124A, 124B, 124C	For creation of National Judicial Appointments Commission for recomm-ending appointment of Supreme Court and High Court judges.
100. The Constitution (One hundredth Amendment) Act, 2015	1st Schedule	To provide for giving effect to the acquiring of territories by India and transfer of certain territories to Bangladesh.
101. The Constitution for (One hundred and first Amendment) Act, 2016	246A, 269A, 279A and 7th Schedule	To provide Goods and services (GST).
102. The Constitution (Hundred-second Amendment) Act, 2018	338B, 342A	To give constitutional status to National Commission for Backward Classes.
103. The Constitution (Hundred-third Amendment) Act, 2019	15,16,46	to provide 10 per cent reservation in Govt. jobs and College seats for Economically Backward classes.
104. The Constitution (Hundred-fourth Amendment) Act, 2020	334	to provide for continuing Reser-vation for SC & ST & Spl. provision for Anglo-Indians for another 10 yrs. (up to 2030)

Addendum

Studying The Constitution

I have been a humble student of Constitutional Law and specially of the Constitution of India for the last 72 years (1949-50 onwards). I was also privileged to have seen, as they say, 'in flesh and blood' and later closely interacted with some of the most prominent founding fathers including Baba Saheb Dr. Ambedkar. The Constitution was adopted, enacted and given to ourselves, in our Constituent Assembly, on 26 November 1949. It came into full operation and the new Sovereign Democratic Republic of India was born on 26 January, 1950.

For students of Constitutional Law, the Constitution of India appears as a voluminous and formidable document. Known as the lengthiest Constitution of the world, it is unique in many ways and, unfortunately, there is no easy way to really understand it. Guides are more likely to mislead. The golden rule, therefore , is: when in doubt in any constitutional matter, it is best to consult the Constitution itself. I may narrate the story of a personal experience which for me was shocking. Many many years ago, a candidate—first class first Master's degree holder with a special paper on the Constitution—when asked about certain provisions of the Constitution fumbled. When asked by another member of the Interview Board whether he had ever read or consulted the text of the Constitution, he named some books on the Constitution but honestly admitted that he had on no occasion read or consult the text of the Constitution itself. Perhaps somewhat exasperated, the third member of the Board asked the candidate whether he had seen the text of our Constitution. The reply again was a candid 'no'. That speaks volumes on our education.

Again, it is on account of our bad habit of not consulting the text of the Constitution that we all commit many horrors like talking of and writing on 'impeachment' of judges while there is no provision for 'impeachment' as such, of judges (see article 124(4)). Provision for impeachment is only and only for the President (article 61).

Doubt, Question, Discuss (DQD)

Cogito ergo sum meaning 'I doubt, therefore, I am' is the famous saying of the distinguished French philosopher and mathematician, Rene Descartes. Generally, students are expected to accept what they read or are taught. But, while pursuing my constitutional studies, my teachers encouraged me to doubt, to disagree and to question. I must admit that I have always learnt more by questioning and by being questioned.

About advice, someone said: 'A word of advice: never give it'. Nevertheless, it may be suggested to budding jurists and lawyers in law schools and universities to embark on their studies with an open, doubting and questioning mind and not accept anyone , including the present writer, without due scrutiny and full satisfaction on facts and law.

Vade vade jayate tattvabodha. It is through debate and discussion that one gets to know the quintessential truth. Knowledge grows through interaction of minds. A practical advice to law students may be to form informal study groups from among themselves to critically examine and contemporaneously discuss current issues of constitutional importance including select High Court and Supreme Court judgements, varying interpretations of constitutional provisions and constitutional controversies in the process of working the Constitution. It is wrong to think that court judgements including those coming from the highest court, cannot be disagreed with or criticised in media or academia. Even the Supreme Court may go wrong. Since the law declared by the Supreme Court is binding on all 'courts' in India (article 141) and there is no appeal against its decisions, there may be some finality attributed to them but no infallibility can be claimed for them. All the high government functionaries including the President, Ministers and the judges themselves, take oath by the Constitution and therefore, to judge the validity of any act, whether of the executive, of the legislature or of the judiciary, the point of reference has to be the Constitution. The Constitution clearly defines, demarcates and delimits the jurisdictional limits and areas of responsibility of the three organs of the State. None of them can claim supremacy except in its own sphere. For example, the independence of the judiciary is, no doubt, important but so is the independence of the legislature. The system works on the principle of checks and balances.

What, Why and How (WWH)

Every Constitution represents the vision and values of its founding fathers and masters it was being made and after the Constituent Assembly was wound up and the Constitution became operative in 1950, it continued to be made (see the volume titled 'Constitution Making Since 1950').

The Constitution gets meaning and content only from the manner in which and the people by whom it is operated, the effects it acquires from how it is worked, the amendments that are made by the constituent power, the interpretations given by courts of the land and the conventions and practices that grow around it in the actual process of its woking.

Sometimes, in the curriculum of law studies, IPC, CrPC, Law of Evidence etc. are taken up first and Constitutional Law is relegated to subsequent years. It needs consideration whether for beginners in law, the best course may be to begin with getting acquainted with the Constitution which is the foundational law and with reference to which all other laws are tested for their validity. And, for studying the Constitution, traditional wisdom tells us at first raise the conceptual questions: What is a nation's Constitution, why it is needed and how it works.

Since the edifice of every nation's Constitution is built on the plinth of its past, for meaningfully studying it, it is necessary to know the country's constitutional history. Also, we must be aware of the reasoning and intent in the minds of our Constitution makers behind every provision of the Constitution. Hence, the relevance of details of the story of Constitution-making , Constituent Assembly Debates, reports of various committees etc. To give a practical example, I was for long intrigued by the common use of patently wrong terms like the Central Government, Centre-State Relations, Central Laws, etc. Even the official report of the Sarkaria Commission was titled as the Report on Centre-State Relations. The Constitution-makers discarded the concept of centre and the Constitution itself does not use any of the terms involving the concept of centre. Instead the concept and the term used by the Constitution makers was that of the Union. India, that is, Bharat, is described as a Union of States (article 1) and a whole Part of the Constitution is headlined as 'Relations Between the Union and the States'(Part XI, articles 245-263). The objection to the wrong use of the word 'Centre' for 'Union' is not mere semantic or indulging in sheer tautology.

Words are a very powerful things; those in the legal fraternity know it more than all others. When a word is uttered, an image is created in the mind of the listener. 'Centre' is a point in the middle of the circle while 'Union' connotes the whole 'Circle'. In the context of a nation's political structure and distribution of powers, when we say 'Centre' the image created is that of centre of power and authority against the States in the periphery while in the case of the use of the word 'Union', we see the whole nation with the States as its integral parts; the relationship being one between the whole and its parts. It needs to be realised that a great deal of damage has been done to relations between the Union and the States as a result of the patently wrong use of the word 'Centre'. But, how and why did it happen? I got an answer from the constitutional history of India.

Government of India Act, 1935 envisaged a federal structure for India with provincial autonomy and limited responsible elected government. As we know, the federal part of the 1935 Act never came into operation and the Government of India Act, 1919 continued to operate at All India level. The 1919 Act provided for Central Legislature, Central Laws, Central Government etc. In fact, it was clearly stated by the Joint Committee on Constitutional Reforms that the Government of India under the 1919 Act remained 'unitary and centralised'. Even after the Indian Independence Act, 1947 and commencement of the Constitution in 1950, the colonial hang over of the 'Centre' continued to dominate the operators in the GOI secretariats in South and North Blocks. Since the babus were forced by the colonial habit to use the wrong word, we all followed and the fallacy continues to cause misunderstandings and damage to Union-State relations. Instead of relationship between parts (States) and the whole (Union), it is seen as a relationship between the Centre of authority (GOI) and States in the periphery.

I recall one more story which may be of interest to law students of all ages. Some 50 years back, a brilliant young lawyer wanting to specialise in Constitutional Law came seeking advice on a suitable topic for a research project. It was suggested to him to simply prepare an annotated list of all the articles of the Constitution which could be varied or amended by Parliament without recourse to the procedure in article 368 which is the specific article dealing with 'Amendment of the Constitution'. After examining the list, consequences could be drawn. Not only the amendments under articles 2-4 and 169 which were clearly said not to be regarded as amendments under article 368, there were many provisions of the Constitution which were so worded as to remain valid only 'until'/'unless' Parliament provided otherwise. e.g. Even for the Supreme Court, the number of judges provided in article 124 was to be 'until Parliament by law prescribes a larger number...not more than seven'.

Some 25 years later, when the same person had come to occupy a very high position in the Judiciary, we met at a high level dinner. Amidst the dignitaries present, he recalled how the advice had made him read the entire text of the Constitution word-by-word which otherwise he would have never done. That gave him tremendous advantage over his colleagues. The results of research were personally astounding for him. The number of articles that in effect were amendable without being considered 'amendments' was very large, each with a story of its own.

More, some other time.